As a 15-year-old Kevin Berry swam at  Rome. Four years later he conquered winning an Olympic gold medal in the 200-metre butterfly at the Tokyo Games. During his illustrious swimming career he broke twelve individual world records and also won three Commonwealth Games gold medals.

Better known as a photographer and sports marketer, *2000 Things You Didn't Know About the Olympic Games* is Kevin's first foray into book publishing. The project grew out of his great love of the Olympic movement.

Bob —

I hope you enjoy these stories about the Olympic Games — with an Aussie slant.

Regards
Kevin

2000

THINGS YOU DIDN'T KNOW ABOUT THE
OLYMPIC GAMES

KEVIN BERRY

First published 1998 in Ironbark by Pan Macmillan Australia Pty Limited
St Martins Tower, 31 Market Street, Sydney

Copyright © Kevin Berry 1998

All rights reserved. No part of this book may be reproduced or transmitted in any form or by any means, electronic or mechanical, including photocopying, recording or by any information storage and retrieval system, without prior permission in writing from the publisher.

National Library of Australia
cataloguing-in-publication data:

Berry, Kevin, 1945– .
2000 things you didn't know about the Olympic Games

ISBN 0 330 36115 5.

1. Olympics. 2. Olympics – History. I. Title.
796.48

Typeset in Gill Sans Light by Midland Typesetters
Printed in Australia by McPherson's Printing Group

ACKNOWLEDGEMENTS

I am greatly indebted to many people for their kind assistance in preparing this book.

Harry Gordon, the doyen of Australia's Olympic historians and author of the definitive work, *Australia and the Olympic Games*, has been a wonderful 'sounding board' for me while preparing this book. His guidance and advice is much appreciated and his friendship is greatly valued.

Jim Webster, media director of the Australian teams at the Barcelona and Atlanta Games and a long-time journalist friend, collaborated in researching some of the items included in this book.

Ian Heads, my room mate at the Atlanta Games and someone with whom I share a love of sporting nostalgia, has been a source of much inspiration to me. I thank him for the time he has devoted to leading me down the path to publishing this book.

I have also used the following publications to gather some of the information contained in this work: *The Complete Book of the Olympics* by David Wallechinsky; *Australians at the Olympics* by Gary Lester; *Aussie Gold* by Reet and Max Howell and *Australian and New Zealand Olympians* by Graeme Atkinson.

And to my good friend and partner, Libby Thomas, I say 'Thank You'. You have put up with a lot over the past few years with my constant ravings about *the Olympics*. I think you now must know more about the Games than most Olympians. This book is dedicated to you.

FOREWORD
BY MURRAY ROSE

The most magnificent boat ever to have sailed on Sydney Harbour is gently launched on its maiden voyage. A sudden gust of wind catches the sails and it heels over, picking up speed. My delight turns to panic as my toy yacht heads for open water.

An old bloke fishing from a dinghy nearby hears my desperate cry and quickly puts down his handline to grab the little boat. He rows back to the beach and I wade into the water to meet his outstretched hands and clutch the prized catch to my chest. The man's kind, weathered face is still etched in my mind. 'Can't swim, eh?'

'No,' I shyly reply, 'not yet.'

A moment in time that changed my life for ever. From this brief incident a dream was born to swim fast and to maybe one day represent my country at the Olympic Games.

The history of the Olympic Games has been chronicled in a library of books but the Olympic spirit can never be captured by facts and statistics. The heart and soul of the Games can only be revealed by the athletes and their individual stories of anguish and triumph. These stories are an integral part of the human quest for greatness.

The defining image I have of Kevin Berry is of him straining with all his considerable strength to swim butterfly against a fixed tether in the Townsville Tobruk Pool during our preparation for the Rome Olympics. Alongside him is his good friend and arch rival Neville Hayes. The two young Australian swimmers battled for hours in a gruelling test of survival. They earned a reputation for toughness on the long journey to Olympic glory and the affectionate pseudonyms 'Punch' and 'Judy' (Kev was Judy).

In *2000 Things You Didn't Know about the Olympic Games* Kevin Berry has compiled an extraordinary collection of Olympic anecdotes. He has uncovered little-known stories of heroics and humour, pain and ecstasy. The common thread is the ability of the human spirit to endure with honour. This conviction goes to the very core of the Olympic experience—that to enter the arena and complete what one sets out to do is the highest form of courage.

The Olympic dream is not a remote ideal, it can touch and inspire each of us at any time. Kevin takes us into the world of the Olympic Games with an insight that excites the imagination to ride its own chariot of fire.

Murray Rose, 1998

PREFACE

Like many Australians, my initial experience of the Olympic Games was way back in 1956 when the Games came to the southern hemisphere for the first time.

As a young boy, sitting in a classroom at De La Salle College, Marrickville, I listened on radio to the magnificent performances of our swimmers in the pool in Melbourne and their deeds ignited a spark in me. The glow from this spark led me to a swimming pool in Chippendale, then to a swimming club, the Pyrmont Amateur Club, and eventually to the legendary coach Don Talbot.

Four years on from Melbourne I found myself on the same team as most of the stars from the '56 Games and at 15 years of age I swam in the final of the 200-metre butterfly in Rome.

But it was not just what happened in the pool of the Eternal City that caused me to become an Olympophile. As that young boy, standing in the recreation hut of the Olympic village, I saw Russian track and field athletes dancing with American basketballers. 1960 was the height of the Cold War, but there in front of me were athletes from the two major protagonists of this war enjoying each other's company and participating in the true spirit of the Olympics. I said to myself then, 'If this is what the Olympics is all about, I want to be part of it.'

That was thirty-eight years ago and I feel the same way today as I did then.

This book is the result of much research into some of the more unusual and interesting facets of the Olympic movement. It has involved many hours of exploration and attention to all matters Olympic, and most certainly has been a labour of love.

The Olympic Games are something very special. They are

surrounded by a special aura and you have to experience a Games before you know this feeling. Fortunately for Australians, the Games are returning to this country in the year 2000. When IOC President Samaranch announced on that magic night in September 1993, that 'The winner is Sid-en-ey' I cried for over an hour. As the sun rose over the future Olympic City the following morning I looked in the mirror and asked the question, 'Why am I crying?' The simple answer came to me, 'If I can't cry today, I never will!'

The following 'capsules' are just a brief glance at part of the fabric which makes up the Olympic Games. I hope you enjoy the glimpse.

Kevin Berry, 1998

MARATHON DISTANCE

Since 1908, the distance for the marathon race has been the curious length of 42.195km, or 26 miles 385 yards.

In that year, for the first London Games, the race was to start at Windsor. But as the British royal family were anxious for their children to see the start, the starting line was moved to the private grounds of Windsor Castle.

The distance from the Castle to the Shepherd's Bush stadium finishing line was 26 miles 385 yards and it has remained the standardised distance for the marathon.

The 400-metre hurdles is among the toughest of athletic events, demanding tremendous stamina as well as classic technique. Considered too hard for women, this event was not allowed to be contested until the 1984 Los Angeles Olympics. The inaugural event made history in more ways than one, for Nawal El Moutawakel led from start to finish. She was the first woman from an Islamic nation to win an Olympic medal and Morocco's first-ever gold medal winner.

STAN ROWLEY

Stan Rowley has the best record of any male sprinter in Australian Olympic history. He won the bronze medals in 1900, at the Paris Games, in 60 metres, 100 metres and 200 metres.

However, he also won a gold medal that Australia has never officially recognised. Rowley competed in the 5000-metre team event with the winning English team.

In 1900 there were no national teams and athletes competed as individuals. It was not unusual at the time for one athlete to partner another from a different country.

Officially, in Olympic records, Great Britain is recognised as the winner of the 5000-metre cross-country team event and Stan Rowley of Australia was a member of that team.

Mamo Wolde of Ethiopia first competed in the Olympic Games in Melbourne in 1956 when he came last in his heats in both the 800 metres and 1500 metres. He did not compete in 1960 but was back in 1964 when he finished fourth in the 10,000 metres. Then in Mexico City in 1968—twelve years after his first Olympic appearance—he led the marathon into the stadium and kept circling the track until officials finally waved him to stop. Nobody had ever told Mamo what happened at the finish line. But at age thirty-six, he had finally won an Olympic gold medal.

FIRST FEMALE GOLD MEDALLIST

The first female winner in Olympic history was Charlotte Cooper of Great Britain. At the Paris Games of 1900, Cooper won the tennis tournament beating Helene Provost of France 6–4, 6–2. Later in the same day she teamed with Reginald Doherty to win the mixed doubles.

At the turn of the century Miss Cooper was considered the dominant female tennis player in the world. Prior to the Olympics she had won Wimbledon in 1895, 1896 and 1898 and following the Paris Games she won two more Wimbledon titles in 1901 and 1908.

Charlotte Cooper was also a finalist in the first Wimbledon mixed doubles in 1913.

The longest wrestling contest in Olympic history was the middleweight semi-final bout at the 1912 Stockholm Games between Martin Klein of Russia and Alfred Asikainen of Finland. The two men struggled on for hour after hour under the hot sun stopping every half hour for a brief refreshment. Finally, after eleven hours, Klein pinned his opponent but was so exhausted he was unable to take part in the final. The gold medal was won by the Swede, Claes Johanson by default.

BARON PIERRE DE COUBERTIN

Credit for the modern Olympic movement goes to a Frenchman, Baron Pierre de Coubertin, who read of the excavations at the site of the ancient Games, Olympia, and began to dream of the revival of the Games.

He was convinced that not only the French, but people of all countries could benefit from sport and athletic competition. His dream came true when the first Games of the modern era took place in Athens in 1896.

De Coubertin devoted himself and his fortune to the pursuit of his Olympic dream. When he died, virtually penniless, on 2 September 1937, his heart was taken to Olympia where it rests in a special memorial not too distant from the ancient Olympic stadium.

> At the Berlin Games of 1936 all gold medal winners were presented with a one-year-old potted oak seedling which was adorned with the motto 'Grow to the honour of victory! Summon to further achievement!'. It is thought that a few of the oaks are still alive to this day including one taken back to America by the legendary Jesse Owens.

STELLA WALSH

In 1930, Stella Walsh became the first woman to run 100 yards faster than eleven seconds.

Walsh had been born Stanislawa Walsiewicz in Poland in 1911, and moved to the United States as a youngster with the rest of her family. When the 1932 Olympics came around, US track enthusiasts were looking to Walsh to win a gold medal at the Los Angeles Games.

But there was a problem! Walsh had lost her job during the Depression and, unable to find anything else she accepted a job from the Polish Consulate in New York and decided to compete for Poland.

In the 100 yards, she equalled the world record in each of her three races and won the gold medal easily. Four years later, at the Berlin Games, in front of Adolf Hitler, Walsh was beaten by American sensation Helen Stephens.

Stella Walsh settled in Cleveland, Ohio, and in December 1980 her name rose to prominence again. Walsh was shopping in her home town when she was caught in the middle of an armed robbery and fatally shot.

An autopsy was performed and it was only then that an amazing fact came to light. She did not have female sexual organs—Stella Walsh was a man!

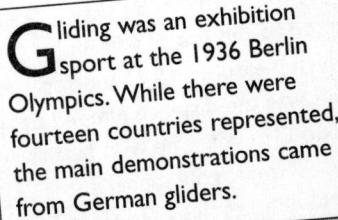

Gliding was an exhibition sport at the 1936 Berlin Olympics. While there were fourteen countries represented, the main demonstrations came from German gliders.

THE OLYMPIC MOTTO

The Olympic motto is 'Citius, Altius, Fortius' which appears under the five interlocked Olympic rings. The motto was conceived by Father Henri Didon, headmaster of The Arcueil School near Paris, France.

Father Didon was born in 1840 and was appointed headmaster of the school in 1890. A preacher and a writer, this Dominican friar had a profound effect on his pupils.

He was one of the first teachers in France to attach importance to physical exercise and organised sports. Arcueil was the first private school participating in interscholastic sports competitions.

In his speech to the students at Arcueil on the day of their first assembly, Father Didon told the assemblage, grouped before him by sports clubs: 'Here is your motto: Citius, Altius, Fortius! *Even Faster, Higher, Stronger.*'

Father Didon came to the attention of Baron Pierre de Coubertin, the founder of the modern Olympics, and was invited to speak at the second Olympic congress, convened at Le Havre.

Didon's topic was 'The Moral Effects of Athletic Sports'.

At the Opening Ceremony of the Tokyo Games in 1964 the Olympic flag was raised to the top of a flagpole which measured 15.21 metres. This was the distance jumped by Mikio Oda when he won Japan's first Olympic gold medal in the triple jump at the 1928 Games.

ODD SPORTS

Cricket was once part of the Olympic Games although, strangely enough, Australia never entered a team.

The gentlemen's game was played at only one Olympics, in 1900 at Paris, and the only two competing countries were Britain and France. Hardly surprisingly, Britain won, 262 runs to France's 104.

'Plunge for Distance' was also another short-lived Olympic event. Contestants began with a standing dive into a swimming pool where they remained motionless for sixty seconds or until they ran out of breath; the length of their dive was then measured.

The event was held at only one Olympic Games—St Louis in 1904. The gold medal went to William Dickey of the United States with a modest plunge of 19.05 metres.

Among other discontinued Olympic sports are croquet, golf, lacrosse, polo, tug of war and rugby. Australia won a gold medal in rugby at the 1908 London Games.

> Motor-boating events were held at the 1908 Olympic Games. There were three classes which were contested but, unfortunately, in each case, only one boat finished and only the gold medal was presented. The open class was won by France while Great Britain took out both the 60-foot and 8-metre classes.

FIRST OLYMPIC CHAMPION

The first recorded Olympic victor was a Greek cook named Corebus who came from the town of Elis. He won the only event contested at the first ancient Games of 776 BC.

There was only one race of approximately 200 metres or one length of the stadium in Olympia, Greece. Corebus' prize was an olive wreath.

The athletes of Elis maintained an unbroken string of victories until the fourteenth Olympics at which time a second race of two lengths of the stadium was added.

In the fifteenth Olympics, an endurance event was introduced in which the athletes went twelve times around the stadium or about 4.5 kilometres.

As time went on other races were included, as were other sports such as boxing and wrestling. Prizes became more elaborate and there were even cases of bribery, corruption and boycotts.

In 1932, at the first Los Angeles Olympics, American football, or gridiron, was played as a demonstration sport. The East played the West and the West won by a score of 7–6. Twenty-four years later at the Melbourne Games, our home-grown sport of Aussie Rules was played as the demonstration sport.

CLARE DENNIS

Australian swimmer Clare Dennis caused a sensation at the 1932 Los Angeles Olympics—and it wasn't because of her swimming ability.

The 16-year-old was almost disqualified after her heat win in the 200-metre breaststroke for wearing a swimsuit which did not conform to international regulations. A protest was lodged claiming her pure silk Speedo showed 'Too much shoulderblade'.

Fortunately, Australian officials were convincing in their arguments and she was allowed to swim in the final, which she duly won in Olympic record time.

The Clare Dennis fracas of 1932 was the first of many swimsuit controversies to have plagued Australian swimming over the past sixty years.

The oldest and youngest male competitors at the Mexico City Olympics of 1968 both came from the same country, El Salvador. The oldest was Roberto Soundy who was a trapshooter and was aged sixty-eight years and 229 days. The youngest was Ruben Guerrero who swam in the medley relay event. Guerrero was only thirteen years and 351 days old. The youngest competitor overall at those Games was another swimmer, Liana Vicens of Puerto Rico. She swam in the 100-metre breaststroke when she was only eleven years and 328 days old.

PRESSURE EVENT—
1992 EQUESTRIAN

We all hear about the pressure of competition at the Olympic Games and it can be perhaps exemplified by what happened in the three-day equestrian event at the Barcelona Games of 1992.

Going into the last day, following the dressage and endurance sections of the competition New Zealand led Australia by 32.8 points. This lead was strengthened following the first two rounds of the showjumping. Australia's Andrew Hoy and Gillian Rolton, and their horses, Kiki and Peppermint Grove, had jumped well but Blyth Tait and Vicky Latta had positioned New Zealand for an almost certain gold medal.

It came down to the last rounds of Andrew Nicholson (NZ) and Matthew Ryan of Australia.

Nicholson had a disastrous round. Riding Spinning Rhombus he knocked over nine obstacles, worth a minus forty-five points.

Ryan, on his mount Kibah Tic Toc, needed to clear every jump if Australia was to win the gold medal.

Despite the huge amount of pressure on him, Ryan had an almost perfect round and cleared all but the last obstacle. This round not only gave Australia the team gold, but also enabled Ryan to take out the individual gold.

> While table tennis is an Olympic sport it was banned in the Soviet Union between 1930 and 1950. The communist regime believed it was harmful to the eyes.

JESSE OWENS

One of the greatest of Olympic champions is America's Jesse Owens.

Owens, the grandson of slaves, was born in Alabama in 1913 and later attended Ohio State University. He became inspired to run fast after a chance meeting in 1928 with Charley Paddock, at that time the world's fastest human!

On 25 May 1935, Owens, competing for Ohio State, took part in a track and field meet at Ann Arbor, Michigan. Before 10,000 spectators Owens set an incredible five world records and equalled another in the space of forty-five minutes.

In the 1936 Berlin Olympics, in front of Adolf Hitler, he won the 100 metres, 200 metres, long jump, and was in the 4 x 100-metres relay. Counting the heats, he competed twelve times in Berlin and finished first each time. He broke nine Olympic records and set four world records.

Owens turned professional a few months after the Games and made his income racing against horses, dogs and motorcycles.

A heavy cigarette smoker all his life, Owens died of lung cancer in March 1980.

For the Munich Games of 1972, the sport of waterskiing was nominated as an exhibition sport. Demonstrations were held in Kiel, the site of the yachting competition, and thirty-six competitors from twenty countries took part. Events were won by some of the best waterskiers in the world including Roby Zucchi of Italy, Ricky McCormick from the United States and Sylvie Maurial of France.

CASSIUS CLAY

At the 1960 Olympics in Rome, the United States had a young, brash 18-year-old from Louisville, Kentucky, representing them in the light heavyweight boxing. His name was Cassius Marcellus Clay.

The young Clay revelled in the atmosphere of the Games. He spent much of his free time meeting competitors from other countries and being photographed with them.

In the boxing ring Clay was in his element. He stopped a Belgian in the second round and went on to defeat the Soviet fighter who had won the middleweight gold medal at the Melbourne Olympics.

His third bout was against Australia's Tony Madigan who was rated a great chance for a medal. The contest was very close and Clay eventually won it but only after a disputed points decision.

In the final, Clay met the fancied European Champion Zbigniew Pietrzykowski of Poland.

For the first two rounds Clay played with the Pole. He danced around Pietrzykowski and avoided every punch the veteran threw at him. In the third round Clay overwhelmed his elder opponent and went on to win a clear and unanimous decision.

Shortly after his triumph Clay returned to his native Louisville and attempted to order a hamburger in a 'whites only' restaurant. When he was refused service he showed the owners his Olympic gold medal. 'I don't give a damn. We don't serve niggers' was the response.

As a result of that incident, Clay went straight to a bridge over the Ohio River and threw his medal into the water.

After embracing the Muslim faith, Cassius Clay changed his

name to Muhammad Ali and became the most famous heavyweight champion in boxing history.

At the 1996 Atlanta Games Ali was presented with a special gold medal honouring his Olympic feat.

The seventy-eighth and last runner to finish the marathon at the 1984 Los Angeles Olympics was Dieudonne Lamothe of Haiti. He finally made it across the line in the very slow time of 2 hours 52 minutes and 18 seconds. Lamothe had also competed in the 5000 metres at the 1976 Montreal Games where he recorded the slowest time for the event in Olympic history. After the eventual fall of Haitian dictator Baby Doc Duvalier, Lamothe revealed that Haitian Olympic officials had threatened to kill him if he ever failed to finish a race.

ABEBE BIKILA

Abebe Bikila is arguably the greatest marathon runner the world has ever seen.

Bikila was born on the outskirts of Addis Ababa in Ethiopia on 7 August 1932. At the Rome Olympics in 1960, running in only his third marathon, he won the gold medal and ran a better time than the mighty Czech Emil Zatopek. And he won running in bare feet!

So unknown was this athlete from Black Africa that when he crossed the line, under the ancient Arch of Constantine, the world's media did not know whether to call him Abebe Bikila or Bikila Abebe.

In a press conference following his victory he was identified as being a member of the Household Guard for Emperor Haile Selassie.

Between 1960 and 1964 Bikila had done nothing extraordinary in the world of athletics. He started at the Tokyo Games in shoes and many thought he was running only out of sentiment. However, Bikila blitzed the field and won by the biggest margin ever in Olympic history, 4 minutes 8 seconds.

He again fronted the starter's gun in the 1968 marathon but had suffered a severe leg injury the year before and was forced to retire at the 10-mile mark.

In 1969 Abebe Bikila suffered spinal injuries in a car crash and was confined to a wheelchair for the rest of his life. He died of a cerebral haemorrhage on 25 October 1973, aged forty-one.

> Gertrude Ederle of the USA and Greta Anderson of Denmark, Olympic swimming gold medallists in 1924 and 1948 respectively, both went on to set English Channel swimming records.

JOHNNY WEISSMULLER

Although there have been many who have played the role of Tarzan in the movies, without doubt the best known is Johnny Weissmuller. But Weissmuller was also a great Olympic champion!

The man who was to later become 'Tarzan the Ape Man' was born on 2 June 1904 in the small Pennsylvania town of Windber. In his late teens he came to the fore as a natural swimmer. He soon revolutionised the front-crawl stroke by turning his head alternately from side to side to breathe.

While it was the great Australian Dawn Fraser who became the first woman to break the one-minute barrier for 100 metres in 1962, Weissmuller was the first man to do so in the early 1920s.

At the Paris Olympics of 1924, Weissmuller won three gold medals in the pool. He took out both the 100 metres and 400 metres and was a member of the triumphant 4 x 200-metre relay. He also won a bronze medal when the USA placed third in the water polo competition.

Four years on, Weissmuller returned to Olympic competition at the Amsterdam Games. He defended his 100-metre title and won a further gold medal in the 4 x 200-metre relay.

In 1929, Johnny Weissmuller turned professional but continued to swim. At age thirty-six he swam the remarkable time of 48.5 seconds for 100 yards.

In 1932 MGM chose him to play the title role in *Tarzan the Ape Man*.

While Johnny Weissmuller won five Olympic gold medals he is best remembered for his movie performances.

> The attaché to the Australian team at the 1992 Games in Barcelona was Maria Samaranch, daughter of the president of the IOC, Juan Antonio Samaranch.

THE OLYMPIC FLAME

The Olympic flame was first used in the modern era in 1928. That year, the flame was kindled in the host city of Amsterdam.

In 1932 it was again ignited in the city of the Games, Los Angeles. However, this was the last time an Olympic flame was kindled in a host city.

The Organising Committee of the Berlin Games, at the instigation of Professor Carl Diem, conceived the idea of rekindling the sacred flame with a torch lit by the rays of the sun. This ceremony was to take place at the site of the original ancient Games in Olympia.

It was also Diem's idea to have the flame carried from Olympia to the host city by torch relay. Once the flame arrives at the stadium, usually well-known athletes or sports figures carry it around the track before climbing a flight of steps (at the Melbourne Games in 1956, this athlete was the famous distance runner, Ron Clarke) they then light the cauldron, which burns continuously during the period of the Games.

This tradition was broken at the Barcelona Games when an archer was used to light the sacred flame.

The sport of lacrosse was played at two Olympic tournaments, in 1904 and 1908. Each time there were only two teams represented and Canada was victorious on both occasions. In 1904 they defeated the USA and four years later beat Great Britain by a score of 14–10. Lacrosse was also shown as a demonstration sport in Amsterdam in 1928, Los Angeles in 1932 and London in 1948.

MARK SPITZ

Mark Spitz was the new wonderboy of swimming when he made his first appearance at Olympic competition. The year was 1968 and the American teenager brashly predicted that he would win six gold medals in the pool at Mexico City. He won two, in relays!

Four years later in Munich, Spitz made no predictions. He had learned to keep his mouth shut and decided to let his actions do the talking.

His first event was the 200-metre butterfly and he won it easily, in world-record time. The four-year burden he had carried was broken!

Spitz went on to win three more individual gold medals—the 100-metre freestyle, 200-metre freestyle and 100-metre butterfly. He also won a further three golds in relays becoming the first person in history to win seven gold medals in one Olympic Games.

Several days after Spitz's last gold medal a group calling themselves the Black September massacred members of the Israeli team. Because of his Jewish background, Spitz was whisked out of Munich and back to the USA. After Munich, Spitz retired and made a fortune in endorsements.

Prior to the Barcelona Games he flirted with the idea of making a comeback but reality caught up with him.

In all, Mark Spitz's Olympic career netted nine gold medals, a silver and a bronze.

> Great Britain's Gillian Sheen won the gold medal for the women's foil event at the 1956 Melbourne Olympic Games. However, there were hardly any members of the British press on hand as they considered fencing a 'minor' sport and Sheen had not been expected to do well.

NADIA COMANECI

Prior to the 1976 Olympics, no gymnast had ever been given a perfect score of 10 in competition. But then along came Nadia Comaneci and during what is remembered as the 'perfect week in Montreal', this petite 14-year-old recorded six such scores.

Comaneci was born on 12 December 1961 in Gheorghiu-Dej, Romania, and was 'discovered' as a gymnast at the age of seven. She was Romanian champion when only twelve and at the European Championships of 1974 she won four gold medals.

At Montreal, Comaneci won the asymmetrical bars with a perfect score of 20, won the beam, finished third in the floor exercises and fourth in the vault. She also helped Romania to the silver in the team competition.

In the combined exercises she was superb! She dropped no more than 0.25 points on any of the four exercises and won easily.

Nadia Comaneci competed at the Moscow Games of 1980 and won a further two gold and two silver medals. She now lives in the United States and visited Australia in early 1994 for the World Gymnastic Championships.

In 1948 the Turkish wrestling team won a total of six gold medals, four silver and one bronze. The national government was so overwhelmed by this success that they awarded the medallists gifts, some of which included money. By accepting these gifts the athletes lost their amateur status and were thus ineligible to compete at future Games.

AL OERTER

Australians are very justifiably proud of our greatest Olympic champion, Dawn Fraser. Dawn won three gold medals, at three consecutive Games, in the same event, the 100-metre freestyle.

But the Americans have a champion who won the same event at four Olympics. His name is Al Oerter and between 1956 and 1968 he reigned supreme in the discus event.

Oerter was only a 20-year-old when he came to Melbourne for his first Olympic Games. Yet he easily won the gold medal.

At the Rome Games in 1960, he threw the discus beyond the world record while casually warming up for the qualifying round. Needless to say, he won the event with consummate ease.

In 1964 at Tokyo, he had his toughest-ever fight to win. Oerter had developed a cervical disc injury, then less than a week before his event he tore a rib cartilage in training. And he had to face Czechoslovakia's new world record holder, Ludvik Danek.

Oerter trailed Danek until the fifth round. He stepped into the circle and gave it everything he had. The discus sailed to 61.31 metres and Oerter had his third gold medal.

At the Mexico City Olympics America had the world record holder in Jay Silvester. Oerter let fly with a monster throw and when measured it turned out to be the winning distance. He had thrown the discus 64.78 metres which was one and a half metres further than he had ever thrown before. With this win he became the first track and field athlete to win four gold medals in the same event.

> The highest score in an Olympic soccer match was the 17–1 defeat of France by Denmark in 1908. During that game the Danish centre-forward, Sophus Nielsen, scored ten goals.

JOHN DAVIES

John Davies is perhaps one of the least known of the many great Australian champions. Yet he holds a unique record in Olympic history that will never be broken: he was the last Olympic champion to use the butterfly arm action to win a breaststroke event.

Davies was successful in taking out the 200-metre event at the Helsinki Games of 1952. Following these Games, two distinctly different events were contested: the traditional breaststroke and the new butterfly stroke.

Davies had studied in America prior to the 1952 Games. He returned there after his victory and married Marnie Follinger.

In 1959 he graduated from Law School at the University of California. For twenty-five years he was a top trial lawyer in Los Angeles and in 1986 President Ronald Reagan appointed him to the United States District Court.

Judge John Davies was the judge who adjudicated during the second controversial Rodney King trial in 1993.

The first brothers to win Olympic medals in track and field were the Irishmen Patrick and Con Leahy. Back at the first part of the century they represented Great Britain and in 1900 Patrick won a silver in the high jump and a bronze in the long jump. In 1908 Con placed second in the high jump.

FIRST MODERN OLYMPIC CHAMPION

The first Olympic champion of the modern era was an American, James Connolly.

In 1896 Connolly dropped out of Harvard University and sailed off to Europe. At the time he was the reigning US triple jump champion.

After arriving in Athens he settled in for a good night's sleep, only to be woken at four o'clock the next morning by a brass band.

To his horror Connolly discovered that the Olympics were about to begin rather than in twelve days' time.

He had overlooked that the Greek calendar was different.

That afternoon James Brendan Connolly strode out onto the stadium and easily won the triple jump. He thus became the first Olympic champion since the boxer Barasdates of Armenia in AD 369.

Incidentally, Connolly did two hops and a jump, which was allowed in those days, rather than the traditional hop, step and jump.

After the Olympics he became a well-known writer and was, ironically, invited back to Harvard University to lecture in literature.

> At the Antwerp Olympics in 1920 Great Britain beat Belgium in the final of the water polo competition. However, the victory ceremony was delayed for some days as the band refused to play the British anthem and officials would not raise the Union Jack.

THE CAFFEINE KID

One of the strangest and most controversial issues in Australia's participation at the Olympics surrounds the performance of modern pentathlon athlete Alex Watson at the 1988 Seoul Games.

Modern pentathlon comprises five sports—riding, fencing, swimming, shooting and running. These events are held over five consecutive days and points are awarded for each performance.

Watson had competed at the Los Angeles Games four years previously and finished a creditable fifteenth in the individual competition.

At Seoul, after four days of competition, he was in twelfth position and had only one discipline to go, the cross-country run. He had been given a random drug test during the fencing day of competition and it had returned a 'positive' swab. His second sample was then tested and it, too, was positive. The drug of abuse was named as caffeine.

Watson appeared before the IOC Medical Commission and claimed the only way the caffeine could have been in his system was through the coffee he had drunk. The Commission did not accept this view and he was disqualified from the competition. He was ordered from the Olympic village by Australian team management and put on a plane back to Australia.

Watson got off the plane at Hong Kong and returned to Seoul. There he held a press conference claiming his drink had been spiked by a Romanian official.

Upon returning to Australia after the Games Watson was given a two-year ban by his international federation and an automatic life ban by the Australian Olympic Federation. This was later reduced to two years. All along, Watson maintained his innocence and went to great lengths to show how the coffee he had drunk on that fencing day could have produced the results in his test.

Alex Watson continued to compete and made the Australian team for the Barcelona Games. He will be the Sports Director for modern pentathlon at the Sydney Olympics.

The fencing competition at the 1924 Paris Olympics literally flowed on afterwards. Insulted by an incident during the Games, Hungary's Italian-born fencing master, Italo Santelli, challenged Italy's team captain Adolfo Contronei to a real duel. Government permission was obtained, but before the contest Santelli's son Giorgio invoked the 'code duello' which allowed him to fight in his father's place. After two minutes of duelling, the younger Santelli slashed Contronei deeply on the side of the head, winning the duel and avenging his father's honour. He later moved to America where he became the US national fencing coach.

MALLIN–BROUSSE BOXING IN 1924

The middleweight boxing event between Harry Mallin of Britain and Frenchman Roger Brousse in 1924 provided one of the greatest controversies in Olympic history.

The defending champion, Mallin claimed Brousse had bitten him on the chest. The referee ignored him and awarded the bout to the Frenchman. A protest was lodged and an examination showed that Mallin had most definitely been bitten.

The Jury of Appeal disqualified Brousse and the following night Mallin won his gold medal bout among much catcalling from the French spectators.

In 1992, Marcus Samuel of Nauru was one of the top ten lifters in his weight category. The problem was that his home country did not have a National Olympic Committee. To overcome this and gain entry to the Barcelona Games, Samuel acquired citizenship of a neighbouring Oceania country, Western Samoa. He placed a very creditable ninth. In 1994 Nauru was admitted into the Olympic movement.

CYCLING AT MONTREAL

The first time cycling was held outdoors at an Olympic Games was at Montreal in 1976. The team from Czechoslovakia got off to a bad start. All their wheels and spare tyres were inadvertently picked up by garbage collectors and fed into a rubbish compactor.

Nevertheless, they managed to obtain new gear and one of their team, Anton Tkac, went on to win the 1000-metre sprint title. He beat the sentimental favourite, Daniel Morelon of France, to take out the gold medal.

The Dragon class yachting at the 1960 Rome Olympics had two famous competitors. The gold medal was won by a crew containing 20-year-old Crown Prince Constantin of Greece. A member of the Philippine crew was Francisco Gonzalez who gained dubious notoriety four years later. In 1964 he shot the pilot of a commercial airliner in California causing the death of forty-four people, including himself. Gonzalez had taken out a $100,000 flight insurance policy before boarding the aircraft.

SABRE EVENTS AT 1924 PARIS GAMES

The sabre events at the 1924 Paris Olympics got out of hand. The Italian fencer Oreste Puliti was enraged at accusations made by Kovacs, a Hungarian judge, and having said so, was disqualified. With that the rest of the Italian fencers walked out.

Two days later the Italian fencer and the Hungarian judge ran into each other at a music hall and had to be pulled apart. Further words were exchanged and a formal duel was proposed.

Four months later the Olympic fencer and the judge slashed away at each other for an hour before being separated by spectators who had become concerned about their wounds. Their honour restored, the two men shook hands and made up.

At the 1976 Montreal Olympics, the hero of Japan's gold medal win in the gymnastic teams event was Shun Fujimoto. He broke his leg at the knee while finishing his floor exercise routine but hid his injury and went ahead with his side horse performance. Then came the rings! He completed a successful routine but he then had to dismount. Landing on his feet in intense pain, Fujimoto compounded his injury by dislocating his knee. Finally he had to withdraw from the competition. Asked years later if he would ever go through pain like that again, he replied without hesitation: 'No'.

KATHY WATT

Kathy Watt was among the smallest of Australia's team members at the 1992 Barcelona Olympics—standing just 1.59 metres and weighing just 50 kg. But she was also among the toughest. The 27-year-old cyclist from Warragul in Victoria decided to go for broke halfway through the final 16.5 km stage of the individual road race. The pack didn't imagine she would hold on, but the harder they chased, the harder she rode, finally winning Australia's first gold medal of the Games. She said later, 'I had always been taught to be aggressive... to fight.'

In the individual pursuit event on the track, Watt led for the first two kilometres before running out of energy. She settled for the silver medal, just 1.685 seconds behind the winner, but with that result she equalled the finest performance of any Australian in Barcelona.

Perhaps the greatest Australian swimmer never to have won Olympic gold was Victorian John Marshall. Between 1950 and 1954 he broke an amazing twenty-eight world freestyle records. While competing at three Games—London, Helsinki and Melbourne—his best result was a silver medal in the 1500 metres in 1948. Marshall died tragically in a car accident in 1957.

JAPANESE WOMEN'S VOLLEYBALL AT TOKYO

Ten of the twelve members of the Japanese women's volleyball team at the 1964 Tokyo Olympics came from the Nichibo spinning mills in Kaizuku, near Osaka. Their coach was the notorious Horofumi Daimatsu.

Daimatsu was famous for his ruthless methods. He would hit his players on the head; kick them on their hips; insult them; goad them and make them practise a minimum of six hours a day, seven days a week.

Whatever might be said for his approach to coaching, his technique did pay off. The Japanese women lost only one set throughout the whole tournament and took out the gold medal.

While it was the Germans who took out the quadruple sculls in Barcelona (1992), it was the crew from Norway who were the crowd favourites. While everyone else used shells of moulded glass fibre reinforced with carbon fibre, the Norwegians used a good old-fashioned wooden boat with wooden oars. They managed to take out the silver medal.

YACHTING REGATTA IN 1976

Funeral director Allen Warren and partner David Hunt provided a light touch to the yachting events at the 1976 Montreal Olympics.

Their six-year-old Tempest class boat called *Gift 'Orse* was damaged in transit to the Games site and performed poorly during the competition. So after the final race, Warren and Hunt took some acetone and a flare and set the boat on fire.

'She went lame on us,' said Warren, 'so we decided the poor old 'orse should be cremated.'

Of interest in that particular class of yachting in Montreal was a young Dennis Conner who went on to win The America's Cup in 1980. He is also remembered as the skipper who lost the Cup for America to the Alan Bond syndicate in 1983.

Today, we are used to our swimming events being held in magnificent 50-metre pools. But the first Olympic competitions were held in the open sea (1896 and 1906); in the River Seine (1900); and in an artificial lake (1904). The first time a pool was used was when a 100-metre-long pool was constructed inside the track at White City Stadium (London). The first 50-metre pool came in 1924.

DIFFICULT URINE SAMPLE

The Olympic middleweight boxing champion in 1968 was English bricklayer Chris Finnegan. But his most difficult challenge in Mexico City did not happen in the ring but rather after the final bout. It was then he was asked to produce a urine sample and he had great difficulty.

People turned on water taps, whistled and generally urged him on with words of encouragement. He even drank several glasses of water but nothing happened. He then turned to his favourite drink, beer, and downed four pints of the amber liquid but still no result.

After giving a TV interview Finnegan went off to a restaurant for a meal accompanied by two Olympic officials with the necessary collection equipment.

Finally, at 1.40 a.m., the Brit jumped up and said he was ready to deliver. The officials and Finnegan headed for the bathroom where he finally produced the required sample.

The test proved negative.

Competitors in the steeplechase event at the 1904 Games had to perform some quite unusual tasks. These days we are used to seeing runners in this event going over the water jump but in St Louis they were required to scramble through suspended open-ended barrels. Film footage exists of this amazing requirement and it is something to behold.

BILL NORTHAM

The Japanese called him 'Ogesan', or the old man. Back home he was known as the Golden Grandpa. He was Bill Northam and at age fifty-nine, this grandfather of five became Australia's oldest Olympic gold medallist.

At the 1964 Tokyo games Northam and his crew of Peter O'Donnell and James Sargeant captured our first-ever Olympic gold medal in the sport of yachting. Sailing the elegant yacht *Barrenjoey*, they won the 5.5 metre class.

Years after his victory the wily old sailor credited much of his success to the daily supply of whisky he consumed. It was rumoured that Bill drank at least a bottle each day! Northam was later knighted for his contributions to the community.

In 1920, a young US Naval lieutenant by the name of Nat Pendleton lost the gold medal on a disputed decision in the heavyweight division of freestyle wrestling. He later went on to achieve fame as an actor in Hollywood playing in many comic 'heavy' roles. A team-mate of Pendleton's was Edward Wilkie who was the brother of Wendell Wilkie, the man who ran for President, on the Republican ticket, in 1940.

DAVID THEILE

The period between 1956 and 1964 is considered the golden era of Australian swimming. The names of Fraser, Rose, Crapp, Konrads and many others were household words.

But there is one name which is very rarely mentioned when we remember that golden era. It is that of David Theile, the forgotten man in Australia's proud swimming history.

Theile is one of the few dual gold medallists who won the same event, the 100-metre backstroke, at consecutive Olympics. He won in 1956 and again in 1960. No other Australian male has won a backstroke gold.

Theile would have missed the Olympics had the senate of the University of Queensland not agreed to postdate his scholarship. He was intent on becoming a doctor and would have given up his Olympic ambitions had the university not agreed.

After winning in Melbourne, Theile virtually cut himself off from swimming and devoted all his time to his studies. When he returned to the pool in 1960, very few gave him a chance of even making the Australian team. Australia was well served with backstrokers in the form of world record holder John Monckton and John Hayres.

But he proved the critics wrong. Not only did he gain a berth for Rome but he went on to defend his Olympic title. It was one of the finest performances by an Australian at any Games.

David Theile won another medal in Rome, a silver in the 4 x 100-metre medley relay. He retired four months later.

> There has been only one draw in an Olympic soccer final. This occurred in 1928 when Uruguay drew with Argentina 1–1. The replay was won by Uruguay 2–1.

RUSSELL MOCKRIDGE

The most celebrated cyclist in Australia's Olympic history is not the legendary Dunc Gray but rather a young man from Victoria named Russell Mockridge.

He remains the only Australian to win two gold medals, both won in Helsinki in 1952. The first was the 1000-metre time trial and the other was with his good friend and riding companion, Lionel Cox, in the 2000-metre tandem.

Mockridge almost missed the Games because he refused to sign a bond guaranteeing that he would remain an amateur for two years after the Games.

Although he turned professional in 1953, his career lasted just five more years. While preparing for a tour of Europe, Mockridge was knocked down and killed by a bus.

Competing in the Tour of Gippsland, a 224-kilometre race, he was riding abreast with two other cyclists about nineteen kilometres from the heart of Melbourne when he skidded under the bus.

Russell Mockridge was a mere thirty years of age when he died.

> At the Olympic Games of 1968, Mexico's Felipe Munoz won his country's first swimming gold medal when he took out the 200-metre breaststroke. Munoz's nickname was 'Tibio' which means lukewarm. The reason for this is that his father came from Agunascalientes ('hot water') and his mother came from Rio Frio ('cold water').

JOHN WINTER

John Winter is the only Australian to win an Olympic gold medal in the track and field discipline of high jump. He won this event at the London Games of 1948.

What was surprising about Winter's victory was the elevation he jumped. He won with a height of 1.98 metres (6 feet 6 inches) which was well below the world record. In fact, many of his opponents had consistently jumped 2.03 metres (6 feet 8 inches) in pre-Games competitions. Yet this height of 1.98 metres may have been fate for Western Australia's first gold medallist.

Prior to the Olympics he had won the Irish high jump title with 1.98 metres and in a post-Games event, against the Americans, he again won with 1.98 metres. Two years later, at the Auckland Commonwealth Games, John Winter won the high jump. His jump? 1.98 metres.

Throughout his career Winter had been troubled by a weakness in his right ankle; and after winning in Auckland he retired from active competition at the age of twenty-seven.

It is worth noting that Nick Winter who won the hop, step and jump Olympic title in 1924 and John Winter are not related.

A member of the victorious East German winning handball team at the 1980 Moscow Olympics was Hans-Georg Beyer. He was the brother of 1976 shot-put champion Uwe, who also won a bronze in 1980. To complete a remarkable family trio, their sister Gisela narrowly missed a bronze medal in the women's discus at Moscow.

MAN OVERBOARD

One of the strangest events surrounding Australia's participation at the 1924 Paris Olympics was what happened on the trip over.

In those days, Australia travelled to the Games by sea. The team set off for Europe on the RMS *Ormonde*. Two days out of Colombo, Tom Adrian, the coach of the great 'Boy' Charlton, began to act quite erratically.

Adrian had fought in World War I and had witnessed many horrific sights. He had fought in the Battle of the Somme and had been greatly affected by the death of his good friend and wonderful swimmer, Cecil Healy. While not receiving any physical wounds, Adrian carried many psychological scars. He was a classic victim of 'shell shock'.

Tom Adrian had been watching deck games on board the *Ormonde* when he suddenly turned and jumped overboard. The ship was in the Arabian Sea and newspaper reports of the day said that the waters were shark infested.

It took a full thirty minutes for the ship to stop and circle back to the spot where he was picked up. The strain of the single-propeller circle caused the tailshaft to break and slowed the progress of the vessel. Fearing the swimmers would be late for competitions in England, the team manager, Ossie Merrett, took them off the ship at Toulon and finished the journey by train.

After the incident, Adrian was confined to locked quarters for the remainder of the trip. Upon reaching England, he was admitted to a London hospital and it was there he heard of 'Boy' Charlton's marvellous Olympic victory in the 1500-metre freestyle.

> In the ancient Olympic Games Tisamenos of Naxos won four Olympic crowns between 540 and 528 BC.

THE FLYING DUTCH HOUSEWIFE

Fanny Blankers-Koen had competed for the Netherlands at the 1936 Olympics in Berlin. However, it was not until the post-war Games of 1948 that she stamped her mark on Olympic history.

As a 30-year-old mother of two she reached her peak at the London Games and was easily the dominant female athlete.

Blankers-Koen won four of the nine women's events in London. Her first two came in the sprints, the 100 metres and 200 metres, the first female to win the coveted double. Her third gold came in the 80-metre hurdles and her fourth was achieved in the 4 x 100-metre relay.

This great Dutch athlete held world records in the high jump and the long jump but was unable to compete in these events. The International Olympic Committee had a regulation preventing her from taking part in more than three individual events.

Fanny Blankers-Koen was coached by her husband and in 1949 they toured Australia. It was during this tour that she was beaten by an up-and-coming young Aussie athlete, much to everyone's surprise. The young Australian was Marjorie Jackson.

> Back in the 1920s they did things in a very civilised way. During the running of the marathon at the 1924 Games in Paris, there was a waiter on hand serving drinks to the runners as they stopped to replenish their liquid intake.

MAUREEN CAIRD

One of the biggest upsets at the Mexico City Olympics of 1968 was the victory of Maureen Caird over her fellow Australian team-mate, Pam Kilborn, in the 80-metre hurdles.

Caird was born at Enmore in Sydney in 1951 and as a young competitor she soon established herself as an outstanding all-round athlete. She won her first national junior title, the 80-metre hurdles, in 1966, at the age of fifteen. Over the next two years she retained this title as well as clinching the Australian junior long jump title in 1968 and the pentathlon championship in 1967.

As the Mexico City Games loomed, the selectors looked at the young hurdler and decided to pick her for the team as a second string to world record holder Pam Kilborn.

Caird made it through to the final of the hurdles and it was here she caused one of the biggest boilovers in Olympic history. A poor start by the more experienced Kilborn allowed the Sydney youngster to flash by and take out the gold medal. This was the first time Maureen Caird had defeated Pam Kilborn and she could not have picked a better time and place—the Olympic Games!

In winning this event she wrote her name into the annals of Australian sport. She claimed her victory a mere nineteen days after her seventeenth birthday and thus became the youngest track and field winner, not only in Australian, but in Olympic history.

Maureen Caird's time of 10.3 seconds will stand forever as an Olympic record. From 1972 the distance for the women's hurdle event was increased to 100 metres.

> Australia won no medals at the third Olympic Games held in St Louis in 1904.

JACK LOVELOCK

While Australians consider Herb Elliott's 1500-metre Olympic victory at Rome in 1960 as being the finest metric mile ever run, our cousins across the Tasman would argue the case of one Jack Lovelock.

Lovelock won the 1500-metre event at the famous Berlin Games of 1936. In taking out this race he became the first Olympic gold medal winner at track and field competition for New Zealand.

Jack Lovelock was born in Cushington and attended Timaru Boys' High School from 1924 to 1928. He was an outstanding athlete and represented his school in rugby, cricket, boxing, tennis, swimming and, of course, athletics.

In 1931 Lovelock was awarded a Rhodes Scholarship and entered Oxford University. Immediately he joined the Oxford Athletic Club and in his first mile race he dead-heated, thus earning his university blue. Soon after, he set a British mile record with a time of 4 minutes 12 seconds and this time earned him selection for New Zealand to the Los Angeles Games of 1932.

At his first Olympics he finished seventh in the 1500 metres. However, it was the following year, in a meet in America, that he shattered the world mile record with a time of 4 minutes 7.6 seconds. By winning this race he defeated all the top US milers.

At the London Empire Games of 1934 he won the mile title and in 1935 he had a marvellous win over Glenn Cunningham, the new world record holder.

When Hitler's Berlin Games took centre stage in 1936 the most eagerly awaited race was the 1500 metres. Many fine athletes lined up for the final including not only Lovelock and

Cunningham but also Luigi Beccali from Italy, the 1932 Olympic champion.

More than 110,000 spectators watched the final. For the first three laps there was much jockeying taking place, and at the start of the last lap Lovelock found himself in fourth position. But it was then he took off. Knowing his opponents' finishing abilities, the Kiwi started his 'kick' a full 300 metres from home. He shot past Cunningham and the Swede Erik Ny, and only Beccali had a chance of defeating the New Zealander.

As he approached the finish line, Lovelock glanced over his shoulder and found the Italian to be in his wake. The winning time of 3 minutes 47.9 seconds was a new world record for 1500 metres.

Jack Lovelock received his Victory Oak Tree, a unique feature of the Berlin Games, from Adolf Hitler. It still grows in the grounds of his old school at Timaru.

> Most Australians remember Jorg Hoffman as the East German swimmer who beat Kieren Perkins at the World Championships in Perth in 1991. However, he had a namesake. In 1904, another Jorg Hoffman won a silver medal in the highboard diving event then swam in the 100-metre backstroke where he also placed second. He is one of only four divers to have completed this unlikely double—of medalling in both diving and swimming.

NICK WINTER

Nick Winter was one of the Manly trio who won all of Australia's gold medals at the Paris Olympic Games of 1924 but is possibly the least well known.

The great 'Boy' Charlton and Dick Eve won their medals in the swimming pool. Winter's success came at the track with his victory in the hop, step and jump or as we know it today, the triple jump.

Winter's gold medal performance was the climax to some of the most exciting scenes ever witnessed in this event. The sportswriters who covered the competition wrote about it for years afterwards. They described the thrilling spectacle of Winter's tussle with the huge Argentinean Bruneto and the 1920 Olympic champion, Tuulos from Finland.

With his final jump, Winter soared to a distance of 50 feet and $11^{1}/_{4}$ inches. This not only won him the gold medal by a mere quarter of an inch but also allowed him to claim the world record which had stood since 1911. So close was the competition that the first five placegetters all beat the previous Olympic record.

The magnitude of Nick Winter's magnificent leap only comes into true perspective when you consider the 1948 Olympic winner did not equal his distance and it was another thirty years before another Australian beat it!

The boy from Manly competed again at the Amsterdam Games in 1928 but finished only sixth in his heat. He retired three years later.

> The first Olympic historian was the Greek Ippias. This ancient writer has given us detailed descriptions of the first athletic festival in 776 BC.

LORRAINE CRAPP

Throughout most of Lorraine Crapp's swimming career her performances were overshadowed by her great rival, Dawn Fraser. It was Dawn who won the 100-metre freestyle at three consecutive Olympic Games. And it is Dawn who is remembered for being the first woman to swim under a minute for the 100 metres.

But it was Lorraine Crapp who was the first to break the magic five-minute barrier for the 400-metre freestyle, an achievement many liken to the first sub-four-minute mile. She did it in Townsville while training for the 1956 Olympic Games.

Crapp, who was born in Jervis Bay, was coached for most of her swimming career by Frank Guthrie. She broke her first world record in January 1954 in winning the NSW State 880-yard championship. Later that same year she travelled to Vancouver, Canada, to contest the British Empire and Commonwealth Games. This was her first major international carnival and she came away from it with two gold medals, the 110 and 440-yard events.

After the Games of 1954 and during 1955 Lorraine Crapp lost form, probably because of a severe ear infection. However, 1956 was to be her best year. During that magnificent twelve months she swam no fewer than eighteen world records, including her sub-five-minute effort in Townsville, and capped off the year with two Olympic gold medals.

Crapp comfortably won the 400-metre Olympic title in Melbourne by 7.9 seconds. To understand just how good this swim was, it must be remembered the second placegetter was the legendary Dawn Fraser.

Lorraine Crapp's second gold came in the 4 x 100-metre

freestyle relay. In this event she combined with Fraser, Faith Leech and Sandra Morgan to finally clinch every female freestyle event at the Melbourne Games.

Following 1956, Crapp continued swimming but she never reached the heights of her performances that year. She attended the Cardiff Commonwealth Games in 1958 where she was overshadowed by Fraser and a new young star by the name of Ilsa Konrads.

Lorraine Crapp finished her swimming career at the Rome Olympics of 1960 by winning a silver medal in the 4 x 100-metre freestyle.

There's an interesting story about Frank Havens who won the 10,000-metre Canadian canoeing event at the Helsinki Olympics! In 1924 his father, Bill, was selected to be a member of the USA's rowing eights to compete in Paris. At the time Bill's wife was expecting their first child so he declined to make the trip to Paris. That crew took out the gold medal and it seemed the Havens family were denied their gold medal. Not so. The child who was born five days after the finish of the Games was Frank—the winner of canoeing gold in 1952.

UNDERWATER SWIMMING

At the second modern Olympic Games, in Paris in 1900, the most unusual event was underwater swimming.

It was decided prior to the competition that two points would be awarded for each metre swum underwater. In addition, one point was added to the scoring of each competitor for every second he stayed below the surface.

Much to the delight of the locals, Frenchman Charles de Venderville won the event, swimming sixty metres and staying submerged for 1 minute 8.4 seconds. Denmark's Peder Lykkeberg stayed underwater for a longer period, one and a half minutes, but only managed to travel 28.5 metres.

This was the first and only time underwater swimming was held at the Olympic Games.

Tug of war was part of the track and field program at the Olympic Games from 1900 to 1920. In 1900 the gold medal was won by a composite Scandinavian team consisting of three Swedes and three Danes. In 1904 the competition was between American clubs and four years later in London, British police clubs were the competitors. At those Games the London City police beat Liverpool police for the gold medal.

THE PRESS SISTERS OF THE USSR

In Australia there have been several notable family combinations that have competed at the Olympic Games. There was John and Ilsa Konrads, who swam in Rome in 1960. The Roycroft family, led by patriarch Bill, have taken part in many Games over twenty or thirty years. And of course the Anderson brothers have won gold medals in yachting, in separate events, on the same day at Montreal.

But on the international stage the Soviet sisters, Tamara and Irina Press, must surely rank as one of the greatest family combinations of all time. Between them these amazing women set twenty-six world records and won a total of five gold and one silver medal in Olympic competition.

The elder sister, Tamara, won the shot-put gold in 1960 and 1964, the discus silver in 1960 and the gold in 1964. Irina won the 80-metre hurdles gold medal in 1960 and four years later took out the track pentathlon title at Tokyo.

Unfortunately for the sisters, when sex tests were instituted at international competition, the careers of both athletes came to an abrupt end. Very little has been heard of the Press 'sisters' since the mid-1960s.

The first Olympic basketball tournament was in 1936 and it was held outdoors. There were twenty-one teams involved. One of the referees was an American named Avery Brundage. Brundage went on to become president of the International Olympic Committee.

1940 OLYMPICS AWARDED TO JAPAN

The ill-fated Olympic Games of 1940 were awarded by the International Olympic Committee to Japan. It was decided the Winter Games would be held in Sapporo and the Summer Games would go to Tokyo. But when Japan invaded China in 1937 and became caught up in that war, the Olympics were taken away from them.

The Winter Games were rescheduled for Garmisch-Partenkirchen, which was the site of the 1936 Games. However, the whole event was cancelled less than five months before the planned starting date following Germany's invasion of Poland in 1939.

The Summer Games had been reawarded to Helsinki but these too were cancelled when Soviet troops invaded Finland. The Finnish capital, Helsinki, was to hold an Olympic festival in 1952 and Tokyo finally got its chance when it staged the first Asian Olympic Games in 1964.

> Ingemar Johansson of Sweden was disqualified in the second round of the 1952 Olympic heavyweight boxing final. The silver medal was withheld due to his 'inactivity in the ring'. Thirty years later he was finally presented with his medal. In 1959 Johansson won the world professional boxing title from the 1952 Olympic middleweight champion, Floyd Patterson of the USA.

TELEVISION AT THE OLYMPICS

Television now takes the Olympic Games to most of the world's population. The money generated by the massive royalties from television coverage virtually provides all the income for the International Olympic Committee and goes a long way towards bankrolling a host city's staging of the Games.

In a first for the Olympic movement, the IOC awarded television rights for two consecutive Games. The Seven Network was granted the broadcast television and subscription television rights to the Summer Olympic Games in Atlanta and Sydney. The cost for these rights was a staggering US$75 million!

This landmark agreement was reached in consultation with the local organising committees of both Atlanta and Sydney. Apart from exclusive broadcast television and pay television rights for both Games, the agreement also gives Seven the 'assigning rights' to both events, allowing the network to on-sell aspects of the coverage to other broadcast and pay television channels in Australia.

It is sometimes stated the first 'Television Games' were the Melbourne Olympics of 1956. This is not correct. Way back in 1936 the events of the Berlin Games were shown on television screens in the host city. Twenty-five large screens were set up in theatres throughout the German capital allowing locals to see the Games free.

> The Secretary-General of the Australian Olympic Federation between 1973 and 1985, Julius 'Judy' Patching, was the official starter for the track events at the Melbourne Olympics in 1956.

HORACE ASHENFELTER

When Horace Ashenfelter won the 3000-metre steeplechase event at the 1952 Helsinki Olympic Games it caused great excitement in the small community of Collegeville, Pennsylvania.

And the person most surprised was Mrs Horace Ashenfelter Sr, the winner's mother. She is quoted as saying, 'Horace has taken second so many times I wondered why he didn't give up running.'

Going into the Games no-one had given 'Ash' much of a chance. The steeplechase was not his specialty and a Russian athlete named Vladimir Kazantsev had run a time eighteen seconds faster than the US war veteran. The Russians were competing in the sporting festival for the first time in forty years and not since Hitler's Berlin Games had the Olympics had such political overtones.

Going into the final of the steeplechase, eight runners had beaten the previous Olympic record in the heats. Ashenfelter took the lead in the third lap followed closely by Kazantsev. They ran abreast all the way until the last lap and it was then, as expected, the Russian made his move.

Coming to the water jump for the last time Kazantsev had difficulty but the American used a method he had copied from the Finnish steeplechasers. He had noted that the Finns took the water jump by hitting the top of the barrier with one foot and then leaping over the water. Knowing he had nothing to lose, the American used this technique and took the jump with ease.

The 29-year-old FBI agent sprinted away from the field and went on to win the event by 6.2 seconds. He became the first US Olympic champion since 1908 to win a race longer than 800 metres.

Ashenfelter attempted to repeat his gold medal performance in

1956, however he never reached the finals. By this time he was thirty-three years old and summed up his performance in Melbourne philosophically: 'It's progress, I guess. The old guys fade away and new ones take their place.'

> Austerity was the name of the Games back in 1948. Coming out of six years of war Britain was still involved with rationing of food and clothing. Competitors were housed in RAF and Army camps for the men and college buildings for the women. A temporary running track was laid at Wembley Stadium, the home of English soccer, and rowing events were held on the River Thames. The total expenditure amounted to no more than $1.2 million and a small profit of $20,000 was made.

ELEANOR HOLM

Australia's favourite sporting 'rebel' has to be Dawn Fraser. In a period spanning three Olympiads, 'Our Dawn' managed to get off-side with the Australian Swimming Union on a number of occasions and in 1965 she was banned for life after falling into disrepute with this austere body. (This decision was later rescinded to a ten-year ban but unfortunately Fraser did not compete again on the world stage.)

The United States had their own special 'rebel' and her name was Eleanor Holm.

Eleanor Holm had competed at the Los Angeles Olympics in 1932 and won a gold medal in the 100-metre backstroke event. In 1936 she was selected by the US Olympic Committee to compete at the Berlin Games.

In those days, prior to the popularity and availability of the aeroplane, teams travelled to the Games by steamship and this was the case for the US team. They boarded their ship in New York for their trip to Europe and it was during this voyage that Holm gained her reputation.

Eleanor Holm liked a good time and during the long days on board she got up to all sorts of antics. She played dice with the newsmen who accompanied the team; she consumed champagne in large quantities; and she ignored curfew. In short, she disobeyed the rules.

The result was that Holm was dismissed from the team and she did not get the opportunity to defend her Olympic crown. The winner of the 100-metre backstroke at the Berlin Games was Dina Wilhelmina Senff of Holland.

Many considered the whole incident to be an over-reaction by the US Olympic Committee, however the event turned Eleanor Holm into a celebrity and thereafter she had 'star billing' wherever she went.

BOB MATHIAS

When Robert Bruce Mathias was a youngster in Tulare, California, he was anaemic and for years he had to live on special diets and take iron pills. But Bob Mathias grew up to be one of the greatest Olympic champions of all time, winning the gruelling decathlon event at back-to-back Games in 1948 and 1952.

Mathias was introduced to the decathlon by his coach, Virgil Jackson, early in 1948. Jackson suggested he compete in the ten-discipline event at the Southern Pacific AAU Games in Los Angeles. The young Bob agreed but he was shocked to learn he had only three weeks to prepare. And Mathias had never polevaulted, long jumped, thrown the javelin or run a distance race.

Mathias won the Los Angeles event and a second decathlon in Pasadena. From there it was on to the national championships and US Olympic trials. At those trials the 17-year-old won again and became the youngest ever to make the American track team.

At the 1948 London Games, Mathias was handicapped by being placed in the second half of the draw. His group would finish last, late in the evening on each of the two days of competition.

After the first day's events the 'kid from California' was in third place, a mere forty-nine points behind the Argentinean, Enrique Kistenmacher.

The next day rain pelted Wembley Stadium and Mathias was on the field for almost twelve hours. He huddled under a blanket when he wasn't running, jumping or throwing. He had to polevault in half-light with a wet, slippery pole and it was so dark that officials had to hold flashlights so he could see the take-off line for the javelin.

At the end of the day Bob Mathias had faced up to all the

other twenty-seven competitors from twenty nations and won. He was the youngest track and field athlete to win an Olympic gold medal.

Four years later, at Helsinki, Mathias again mounted the victory dais and this time he won with a massive point score of 7887, more than 900 points ahead of the second-placed competitor, Milton Campbell, a fellow American.

> Equestrian competitor Humberto Mariles Cortes of Mexico, won the jumping gold medal in dramatic fashion at the 1948 London Olympics. The last rider to enter the arena, he needed to incur fewer than eight faults to win the gold medal. This he did clearing every obstacle but the water jump and losing only 2.25 points for being slightly over time. In 1964, 51-year-old Mariles was driving home from a party when another motorist cut him off. At the next traffic lights, he pulled out a gun and shot the man. He was gaoled but was later released by presidential pardon. In 1972 he died in a Paris prison awaiting trial for drug smuggling.

PSYCHING UP

Most athletes who compete at the elite level have special ways they get themselves 'up' before a performance. Some competitors make use of sports psychologists to lift them while motivational speakers are employed by some individuals and teams.

And it is not unusual to see swimmers or track athletes walking around with a portable tape recorder and earphones plugged in and it would be a fair guess to say that on most occasions these recorders would be blaring out loud music to psych the athlete up.

Korea's judo team at the 1988 Olympics had a most unusual method! Team members made periodic midnight visits to a cemetery where they sat alone for an hour before returning to their dormitory to watch tapes of their opponents.

This strange technique seemed to pay dividends as the Koreans won gold medals in both the extra-lightweight and half-lightweight classes.

The IOC awarded the Games for 1984 to Los Angeles only after involved negotiations about financial guarantees usually required from a city hosting the Olympics. Various innovations to protect Los Angeles from a Montreal-like deficit were implemented, not the least of which was the widespread sponsorship deals by private corporations.

1920 ANTWERP OLYMPICS

The 1920 Games were awarded by the International Olympic Committee to Antwerp, Belgium.

The European continent had been ravished by the brutality of the First World War and the resolution to award Antwerp the Games was a conscious decision by the caretakers of this great sporting festival. They were determined to compensate the Belgians for all the grief and suffering that had been inflicted upon them during those terrible years between 1914 and 1918.

The losers of the war, namely Austria, Bulgaria, Germany, Hungary and Turkey, were not allowed to compete.

The principal Belgian organiser was Count Henri de Baillet-Latour who, in 1925, would succeed Pierre de Coubertin as president of the IOC.

The seventh Olympic Games brought together 2606 athletes from twenty-nine nations including a New Zealand team for the first time not attached to the Australian team.

With little money available to run the Games the 1920 Olympics were not very impressive or well documented. An official report does not exist for 1920, only a typed manuscript containing an incomplete list of results.

> East Germany's Roswitha Krause was a member of their handball team which took out a silver medal in 1976 and a bronze medal in 1980. Prior to taking up her handball career, Krause had been a swimmer and was a member of the DDR's silver medal-winning team in the 4 x 100-metre freestyle at the Mexico City Games of 1968.

MARJORIE JACKSON

Marjorie Jackson came from the small NSW town of Lithgow which is located approximately 150 kilometres west of Sydney. She grew up practising her running technique on an oval in the town and sometimes trained at night by the light of car headlights.

In 1949, the great Olympic sprint champion Fanny Blankers-Koen came to Australia to compete. In Sydney she faced the young Jackson. The 17-year-old beat the Dutch housewife twice on the one night and instantly came to the attention of the Australian sporting public.

Jackson's first major overseas competition came the following year. She travelled to Auckland for the 1950 Empire Games and managed to win four gold medals. In winning the 100 and 220 yards she equalled the world records for both these distances.

Marjorie Jackson headed off to the Helsinki Games in 1952. Her clash with Blankers-Koen was being heralded as one of the great races of the Games. Unfortunately, Holland's sprinting mother suffered an injury and withdrew from the semi-finals of the Olympic 100 metres. Thus the long-awaited encounter never eventuated and the 'Lithgow Flash' won easily.

In the 200 metres, Jackson broke the world record in her semi-final and then won the final by an amazing five metres. She would have won another gold medal in the relay except the Australian team dropped the baton on the last changeover.

When Marjorie Jackson returned to Australia she was hailed by crowds lining the streets and roads all the way from Sydney to her beloved Lithgow.

> In 1968 Enrequita Basilo became the first woman to light the Olympic flame.

RUGBY AT THE OLYMPICS

Although Australia won the rugby World Cup in 1991, it is scarcely known that they were once Olympic champions as well.

Rugby union was an Olympic sport in 1900, 1908, 1920 and 1924. It was discontinued because only a small number of countries involved in the Olympic movement played the game.

One of those Olympics provided Australia with a gold medal—the 1908 Games in London.

Australia was on its first tour of the British Isles and part of the itinerary was a match in the Olympic tournament. Originally, three countries were to compete—Australia, Britain and France—but the French withdrew when they were not able to find sufficient players of quality.

The British were not represented by their national team. Instead, they chose the previous year's county champions, Cornwall, to represent the country. Australia went into the 'tournament' with much confidence as they had already beaten Cornwall in their third game on tour by the margin 18–5.

Cornwall were bolstered by the return of three players yet they were still beaten by the Aussies 32–5. This victory earned the plaudits of the hard-to-please English critics who had tended to look disdainfully at the colonials.

One of the stars of the 1908 contest was Daniel Carroll from the St George club who scored two tries in the Olympic 'final'. Carroll had the distinction of winning two Olympic gold medals. He was selected for the United States team in 1920 and they won the title at the Antwerp Games.

Australia only ever competed once at rugby in the Olympics.

> Hockey for women was first played at the Olympics in Moscow (1980). The surprising winner was Zimbabwe.

DUNCAN ARMSTRONG

One of the most amazing scenes on Australian television at the time of the Seoul Olympics in 1988 was the sight of swimming coach Laurie Lawrence as he reacted to the victory of his star pupil, Duncan Armstrong in the 200-metre freestyle.

Laurie 'went ballistic'. He shouted. He screamed. He jumped into the diving pool. And he abused the swimming commentator who tried to interview him immediately after Armstrong's win. Mind you, Duncan's win was something special.

There were three world record holders in the event up against the Australian, and he managed to defeat all of them. Matt Biondi from America held the world mark for the 100 metres. Michael Gross, the favourite from Germany, held the 200-metre record, and Artur Wojdat of Poland was the holder of the 400 mark.

Although a Commonwealth Games champion in 1986, going into the Seoul Games Armstrong was considered as only a slight chance for a minor medal in both the 200- and 400-metre events. However Lawrence devised a strategy by which Armstrong could take advantage of swimming next to Biondi in the final. He told his pupil to swim as close to the powerful American as possible and surf off the lanky Yank for at least the first 100. This Armstrong did to perfection. He then hung on during the third lap and unleashed a final surge over the last twenty-five metres to mow down all the would-be contenders. When the times and placings flashed onto the scoreboard, not only did they register that the Australian had won but that he had set a new world record.

The cries of 'lucky lane 6' could be heard reverberating around the Seoul swimming stadium. It was Lawrence. He was referring to the fact that Duncan had won from lane six as had his butterfly ace at the previous Olympics, Jon Sieben.

LARYSA LATYNINA

When Australians are asked to name the most prolific medal winners in Olympic competition they usually mention great Olympic champions like Dawn Fraser, Betty Cuthbert or Murray Rose.

Some might mention the magnificent American swimmer Mark Spitz, or the remarkable discus thrower Al Oerter. But few will put forward the name of Larysa Latynina. Yet Larysa Latynina has more Olympic medals in her possession than any other sportsperson on earth.

This amazing Soviet gymnast is the owner of nine gold, five silver and four bronze medals accumulated over three Olympiads. Additionally, this tally is supplemented by fifteen European and world titles. At the 1956 Melbourne Games, Latynina won three individual gold medals, a team gold, a silver and a bronze.

Four years later, at the Rome Olympics, the gymnastic events were held at the ancient, but beautiful, Baths of Caracalla. The Russian women's team excelled and took out fourteen of a possible fifteen individual medals. Larysa Latynina retained the title in the individual combined exercise; led the USSR to another gold in the team event; and took out the floor exercises. She also picked up two silver medals on the asymmetrical bars and the balance beam and won a bronze for the horse vault.

By the time Tokyo came around in 1964 the legendary Ukrainian was thirty years of age. While she still performed with grace and technical brilliance she could not match the new innovations of her younger Czech rival, Vera Caslavska. However, Latynina still managed to win the individual floor exercises; helped her country win the team combined event and won a further two silver and two bronze medals.

Larysa Latynina retired in 1966 after revolutionising the sport of gymnastics. She displayed an incredible combination of style, grace and agility, the likes of which had never been seen before. Only two other gymnasts can stand alongside her as the greatest the world has ever seen—her Czech rival Vera Caslavska and the Romanian darling, Nadia Comaneci.

Six months prior to the commencement of the Olympic Games of 1932, not a single nation, apart from the United States, had committed to send a team to Los Angeles. The reason why—with the world in a deep economic depression, countries could ill afford the expense of travel to only the second Games staged outside Europe. What saved the day was an idea by IOC secretary Zack Farmer. He hit upon the concept of an Olympic village where athletes could be housed and fed for only $2 a day. Steamship companies came to the party also by agreeing to cut rates for national teams.

FIRST OLYMPIC BASKETBALL TOURNAMENT

While the sport of basketball is going through a huge growth period in Australia, it made its official Olympic debut at the 1936 Berlin Games. The originator of the game was the American Dr James Naismith and he was present at the opening of the Olympic tournament.

The sport had appeared as a demonstration sport in 1904 and, in a Dutch variation, at the Amsterdam Games of 1928. The Berlin event was held outdoors in a tennis stadium on courts of clay and sand.

During the tournament, the International Basketball Federation passed a rule banning all players taller than 190 centimetres. The United States, which would have lost three players, objected and the rule was withdrawn.

The final was played on a quagmire and players found it difficult to dribble on the wet sand. The US won the gold medal in a low-scoring match against Canada, launching a 63-game winning streak. Mexico won the bronze medal.

> It took Toyokau Nomura of Japan a total of ten minutes and forty-nine seconds to dispose of his five opponents in the half-middleweight division of judo at the 1972 Munich Olympics. By achieving this feat, he took out the gold medal.

SWIMMING AT THE FIRST OLYMPIC GAMES

When competitors 'take to the blocks' for the swimming events at the 2000 Olympic Games they will be competing in a state-of-the-art complex. The Sydney International Aquatic Centre was opened to the public in 1994 and already it has hosted a number of major swimming competitions.

The president of the International Olympic Committee, Juan Antonio Samaranch, upon seeing the venue, declared it 'the best swimming pool in the world'.

The swimmers who took part at the first modern Games, in 1896, were not blessed with such a facility. In fact the idea of tempered water in regulation pools, marked lanes and firm starting blocks was not even thought of.

At the Athens Games, the competitors were taken by launch, off the shore of the Bay of Zea, to the approximate distance of a given race. Swimmers then plunged into the icy waters of the Mediterranean and swam, by whatever stroke propelled them fastest, to the beach.

For the record, Alfred Hajos of Hungary won both the 100 metres and 1200 metres while Paul Neumann from Austria won the 500-metre event. As can be imagined, little credence can be given to the times recorded by the victors.

> The first brothers to win gold medals in the Olympic Games were shooters John and Sumner Paine of the USA. In 1896 John won the military pistol event and Sumner took out the free pistol event.

TUG OF WAR

Competition in the sport of tug of war was held at several of the early Olympic Games.

The rules for this contest were very simple. The first team to pull the other over six feet was declared the winner. If neither team succeeded in doing so in the regulation five-minute time frame, then the one who had pulled the furthest was given the victory.

A combined Sweden–Denmark team won the gold medal in Paris in 1900. Four years later in St Louis, Missouri, the United States filled the first four placings.

Germany won in 1906; Britain took all three medals at London in 1908; and Sweden won in Stockholm in 1912. The British took the victor's crown again at Antwerp in 1920, the last Games at which this event was held.

There are three different disciplines within the sport of fencing: foil, épée and sabre. Only two fencers have gained individual medals in all three at the one Olympic Games. Roger Ducret of France won the gold in foil and silver in épée and sabre at the Paris Games of 1924. In the sparsely supported 1904 fencing events, Albertson Van Zo Post, an American who competed for Cuba, won a foil silver and bronze in the other two disciplines.

THE 1904 OLYMPIC MARATHON

The marathon at the 1904 St Louis Games has gone down as one of the most bizarre events in Olympic history. The course was treacherous. It included seven hills and was run on dusty roads. The temperature was 32 degrees Celsius during most of the race and there was only one water stop.

Among the thirty-two starters was a Cuban who had taken a boat to the United States, lost his savings in a crap game, hitch-hiked to St Louis and arrived at the starting line wearing street shoes, long trousers, a long-sleeved shirt and a beret.

Also entered were two African tribesmen who were in St Louis as part of a Boer War exhibit. One of these Africans survived the heat of the day but did not finish the race as he was chased off the course by two large dogs.

Fred Lorz was the first into the stadium. The American was about to be awarded the gold medal when it was discovered he had hitched a ride in a car for nearly eighteen kilometres.

Lorz's team-mate, Thomas Hicks, was awarded the gold medal but controversy surrounds his victory. It appears that during the race his handlers had given him an oral dose of strychnine sulphate mixed with raw egg white. Later he had more strychnine. If present-day doping laws had been operating back in 1904 there is no doubt Hicks would have been disqualified.

> The winner of the 1976 lightweight judo title at the Montreal Games was the Cuban Hector Rodriguez. He said he took up the sport as a youngster in order to learn to defend himself against his six older brothers.

MAX BINNINGTON

Spare a thought for Australian track and field athlete Max Binnington.

Binnington was selected to compete in the 110-metre hurdles at the 1976 Montreal Olympics. As he lined up for his heat he was full of confidence with a hope of getting through to the next round.

The gun was fired and Binnington took off. But the Aussie thought he heard a second report—the signal for a false start. He relaxed and stopped only to find the rest of the field heading towards the finish tape. There had been no recall gun and no false start!

Binnington appealed and asked for a rerun of the heat but this was denied him.

Max Binnington had 'competed' at an Olympic Games but had done so without clearing a single hurdle. Unfortunately, he did not go to another Olympic competition.

This whole event recalled an earlier incident at the 1972 Games and once again a hurdler had been involved. Gary Knoke stopped in a semi-final of the 400-metre hurdles but at least he had already run in a heat of the race.

> In the team contest in the dressage events of the equestrian at the London Games of 1948, the winners were the Swedes. However, the following year they were disqualified and their medals taken away when it was discovered that one of their members, Gehnall Persson, was not a commissioned officer. Under the rules of the event back then, this was a requirement for competition.

KAROLY TAKACS

In 1938, Karoly Takacs was a member of the Hungarian world champion pistol shooting team. As a 28-year-old he was at the peak of his career anxiously looking forward to the 1940 Olympics which had been awarded to Tokyo.

During that fateful year of 1938, while he was serving as a sergeant in the Hungarian army, a grenade exploded in Takacs' right hand and completely shattered it. Karoly Takacs' right hand was his pistol shooting hand!

So ingrained was the Hungarian's desire to win an Olympic gold medal, he taught himself to shoot using his left hand. Slowly Takacs improved and it was not long before he was again able to shoot in international competition.

Ten years after the disastrous accident which should have ended his sporting career, Karoly Takacs gained selection in Hungary's shooting team for the 1948 Olympic Games in London. And, to complete this amazing fightback, at those Games Takacs won an Olympic gold medal in the rapid-fire pistol event.

Four years later, at Helsinki, this tenacious Hungarian again won the gold medal, finishing just one point ahead of his team-mate Szilard Kun.

Karoly Takacs went to a third Olympic Games, in Melbourne in 1956, however he failed in his quest to win a third gold. He finished only in eighth position but his place in Olympic history was assured.

> John Bertrand, who won The America's Cup for Australia in 1983, won a bronze medal in the Finn class of yachting at the Montreal Olympics in 1976.

MERV WOOD

Australian sculler Merv Wood has the distinction of having competed at four Olympic Games over a period of twenty years, 1936 to 1956. In doing so, he managed to secure a full set of Olympic medals.

Wood competed at his first Games in Berlin as a member of the New South Wales police team which represented Australia in the eights. He rowed at number five in a team which dominated in Australia but was unsuccessful overseas. Rumour has it there was dissension among team members of that eight and this is possibly the reason why Merv took up single sculls following the Berlin campaign.

The war interrupted Wood's international career but in 1948 he was selected for the London Games. The rowing events for this Olympiad were held at Henley, and Wood was successful in winning the diamond sculls. This victory gave him the Olympic title and the first of his Olympic medals, a gold.

In 1952, at Helsinki, Wood lost his title to the great Russian Tjukalov. However, he did finish second thus adding the silver medal to his Olympic collection.

By the time 1956 rolled around, Merv Wood was thirty-nine years of age. During the Olympic trials at Ballarat to see who would gain selection to row at the Melbourne Games, the Sydney policeman came up against newcomer Stuart Mackenzie. Wood was beaten convincingly by Mackenzie and watched at the Games as his conqueror took out the silver medal.

But Wood was not finished with his quest. At the Melbourne Games he teamed up with Murray Riley in the double sculls and had the great satisfaction of finishing third. This placing allowed the quietly spoken Wood to complete his full set of Olympic medals by adding a bronze to his gold and silver.

Merv Wood continued to compete after Melbourne and paired with Mackenzie at the Cardiff Commonwealth Games in 1958 in the double sculls. He was then forty-one years old!

> Olympic rower Henry (Bobby) Pearce was the third generation of one of Australia's most famous sporting families. He was in such form leading into the 1928 Amsterdam Olympics that he was considered almost unbeatable. He showed just how dominant he was in his quarter-final, when a family of ducks passed single-file in front of his boat. He stopped rowing, allowed them to pass, and continued on to beat his English opponent in world record time. In the final, he defeated an American in another world record time. Although he moved to Canada, Pearce represented Australia again in 1932 and won a second gold medal. He turned professional in 1933 and was world champion for twelve years.

SURINAM'S OLYMPIC CHAMPION

Surinam is a small West Indian country located on the eastern coast of South America. It has a population of approximately 400,000 people and only one Olympic-sized swimming pool. It also has an Olympic swimming champion!

At the Seoul Games of 1988 the red-hot favourite for the 100-metre butterfly was the USA's Matt Biondi. He was the world record holder and swimming very well going into the Olympics. But in the final of the 100 'fly, Anthony Nesty from Surinam came through and pipped the American.

This created all sorts of havoc at poolside.

First there was the hunt for the national flag of Surinam. You can imagine the organisers of the Games scurrying around trying to find what surely must have been one of the least known flags in Los Angeles.

Then there was the matter of the national anthem for this small country.

Some believe the actual music played at the medal ceremony for Nesty's victory was not the Surinam national anthem but no-one challenged the orchestra conductor. Urban myth has it that he told his band to play anything. He believed there was only one person at the pool that day who would know the difference and he, Nesty, would not care anyhow.

> The great Finnish runner Paavo Nurmi won the 1500-metre and 5000-metre events at the 1924 Olympic Games in Paris. Not so unusual! Well, it is when you consider the races were held only fifty-five minutes apart.

THE ANCIENT OLYMPICS

The first Olympic Games were held at Olympia, a small town in a fertile valley on the western Peloponnese of ancient Greece. The year was 776 BC.

At the first Games there was only one event, the stade. This running race was approximately 200 metres—being the length of the stadium. The athletes were assisted by starting blocks or 'sills' which were embedded in the surface. The first winner of this event was Corebus of Elis.

The Games developed over the years and many varied contests were added to the program. The maximum number of different events was twenty-three but there were never this many held at any single Games. There were some events only for the youth; chariot and equestrian events; and as well as the traditional running events, there were throwing and jumping events. These latter contests were included as part of the pentathlon.

In 680 BC wrestling and boxing were among events included in the Games. Chariot racing proved to be one of the most thrilling tests of the Olympics. The charioteers, who were professionals, raced over fifteen kilometres in the Hippodrome. The prize for the victor was a simple olive branch. The winning athlete gave thanks to Zeus and his home town was considered in favour with the Gods.

According to Pausanias, the greatest of the ancient Olympians was Theagenes. This wonderful athlete from Thassos was successful in six events over four Olympic Games. It is believed he won a total of 1400 contests in his long career.

People came from all over Greece to watch the Olympic Games but the number of spectators is unknown. The stadium at Olympia held 50,000 people but only males of Greek extraction were allowed to compete. These male athletes competed naked and had oils rubbed over them to protect their skin.

The ancient Olympic Games came to a halt in AD 394 when an army of soldiers from Goth destroyed the sacred shrine at Olympia.

The list of Olympic boxing champions includes Floyd Patterson, Muhammad Ali, Joe Frazier, Teofilo Stevenson, Michael Spinks and George Foreman. But few were better than Hungary's Laszlo Papp. Papp won the middleweight gold medal in London in 1948, the light middleweight gold medal in 1952 and he defended this title in 1956. Then at age thirty-one, he gained permission from the Hungarian government to become the first boxer from a communist country to fight professionally. He won the European middleweight title but the government refused to let him challenge for the world championship. In 1965 he retired undefeated.

WILMA RUDOLPH

Wilma Rudolph was born in Tennessee on 23 June 1940, the twentieth child of her father's twenty-two children. When she was four she suffered from polio, double pneumonia and scarlet fever and from the age of six she wore a brace.

At age eleven the young Wilma began running to exercise her withered body and soon took up basketball. In 1955 she was spotted by the famous American track coach Ed Temple and the following year, at the tender age of sixteen, he placed her on the US Olympic team. At Melbourne she won a bronze medal as a member of the American relay team.

By the time the Rome Games of 1960 had rolled around, Rudolph was the queen of world sprinting. She was chosen to compete in the 100-metre and 200-metre individual events as well as the sprint relay team. When she left for Italy she was the favourite to succeed our own Betty Cuthbert to become the world's fastest woman.

At Rome, Rudolph won the 100 metres in 11 seconds flat. Her time was outstanding and unofficially cut half a second from the Olympic record. But her run was wind assisted and the record was not recognised.

In the 200 metres Rudolph won comfortably in a time of 24.0 seconds. Her nearest rival was Jutta Heine of Germany who finished second in 24.4 seconds.

In the final of the 4 x 100-metre relay the Americans were up against strong competition from the combined German team. Rudolph was chosen to run last for her team and taking the baton from her team-mate, she was three metres behind her German rival. In the final straight, the Tennessee flash raced to the front and showed her individual superiority in winning by three metres.

At Rome, Wilma Rudolph became the first American woman to win three gold medals at a single Olympic Games and became instantly popular as the most stylish athlete on the world scene.

In 1961, Rudolph recorded an official world record of 11.2 seconds for the 100 metres and promptly retired.

Wilma Rudolph was often asked how she learned to run so fast. Her reply was simple. With so many brothers and sisters to be fed, she had to get to the family dinner table very quickly to satisfy her hunger!

> The American who was to go on to become president of the International Olympic Committee, Avery Brundage, finished fifth in the pentathlon event at the Stockholm Games of 1912.

BLACK POWER SALUTE

The 1968 Olympic Games held in Mexico City are remembered for a number of reasons. These were the first Games to be held at altitude. They were the site of Mike Wenden's magnificent double victories in the swimming pool. And they were the venue for one of the greatest athletic feats of all times—Bob Beamon's incredible performance in the long jump.

They will also be remembered for the Black Power salute given by the first and third placegetters in the 200-metre track event.

Tommie Smith and John Carlos were both students at San Jose State College in California when they made the American Olympic team in 1968. Both were members of the Olympic Project for Human Rights movement which was a group of athletes organised to protest the treatment of blacks in the United States.

In the final of the 200 metres, Carlos led early in the race but with sixty metres to go, Smith went by his team-mate and won decisively. Carlos turned to watch Smith and this allowed Australia's Peter Norman to slip by and clinch second place.

Smith's victory caused a sensation but nothing compared to what happened at the victory ceremony. Mounting the dais barefooted, Smith and Carlos bowed their heads and each raised one black-gloved hand in the Black Power salute when 'The Star Spangled Banner' was played.

While Smith and Carlos maintained that what they had done was not a ploy to discredit the American flag or their national anthem, Olympic officials were outraged. The IOC made it known that the pair should be punished and the US Olympic Committee responded quickly. They suspended the two athletes and ordered them to leave Mexico within forty-eight hours.

Meanwhile, the whole incident overshadowed Australia's best male performance in Olympic sprinting. Peter Norman, a 26-year-old physical education teacher and Salvation Army officer, had won an Olympic silver medal.

> George Lyon from Canada was an eccentric athlete who competed successfully in baseball, tennis and cricket and once set a Canadian record in the pole vault. At age thirty-eight he took up golf. Lyon was forty-six when he travelled from Toronto to St Louis for the 1904 Olympic Games. He amused everyone on the golf course with his cheerful energy, singing, joke telling and by occasionally doing handstands. Yet with all this carrying on he reached the final and caused a surprise win over US champion, Chandler Egan. Lyon was awarded a $1500 silver trophy, which he accepted after walking down the path to the ceremony on his hands.

THE MAN WHO COULD JUMP

The International Olympic Committee originally chose the city of Chicago to stage the Games of the third Olympiad but American businessmen successfully changed them to St Louis. There was to be an exposition in that city in 1904 and the entrepreneurs wanted to take advantage of this event.

It was at these St Louis Games that one of the most remarkable athletes in modern sport made his mark on Olympic history. His name was Ray Ewry.

Ewry had contracted polio as a child. In order to compensate for the loss of strength in his legs, the youngster worked on his lower limbs. It wasn't long before he had built up extraordinary power in these legs.

Ray Ewry became an exceptional athlete winning fifteen American titles in the various standing jumps. He made his Olympic debut at Paris in 1900, winning the standing high jump, the standing long jump and the standing triple jump.

At St Louis he repeated his victories thus earning his fourth, fifth and sixth gold medals, an amazing feat considering there had only been a very limited number of Olympic golds awarded up to that date.

In 1908 Ewry again won the standing high jump and standing long jump to bring his Olympic total to eight golds.

With an additional two victories at the 1906 Interim Games in Athens, Ewry won ten gold medals.

There is no doubt Ray Ewry was the greatest standing jumper in history!

Australia went 1–2–3 in both the men's and women's 100-metre freestyle at the Melbourne Olympics.

CHARLEY PADDOCK

In the movie, *Chariots of Fire*, much of the action is centred around the British track and field team at the Paris Olympics of 1924. In particular, the film follows the trials and tribulations of two famous runners, Harold Abrahams, winner of the 100 metres, and Eric Liddell whose religious beliefs forbade him from competing on a Sunday.

However there was another famous runner participating in Olympic competition during that period and he was not British. His name was Charley Paddock and he came from the USA. Many people will remember him as the cocky American in the film.

At the Antwerp Games of 1920, Paddock won the 100 metres. Prior to those Olympics he had stated that he was the fastest man in the world and his victory in this blue-ribbon event proved his point. Over the 200 metres, Paddock placed second but he picked up another gold in the 4 x 100-metre relay.

Four years later, in Paris, this flamboyant character could only manage a second in the 200-metre final but it did stamp him as perhaps the most dominant sprinter of this era.

One of the most amazing sights at the Tokyo track and field events happened at the finish of the 20,000-metre walk. Englishman Ken Matthews won the event after he had failed to complete the distance four years previously in Rome. When he crossed the line, his very excited wife, Sheila, evaded stadium security and rushed onto the track and gave her husband the longest victory kiss in Olympic history.

DICK EVE—GOLDEN DIVER

Dick Eve remains Australia's only Olympic diving gold medallist, having won the high diving event at the Paris Games of 1924.

Richmond Cavill (Dick) Eve was born in 1901 and had an impressive aquatic pedigree. His mother, Fredda, was a member of the famous Cavill family who were without doubt the 'first family' of Australian swimming. The Cavills revolutionised swimming in Sydney and many of them set world records and tackled some of the famous 'swims' around the world. Fred, the patriarch of the family, swam the English Channel and sons Ernest, Percy and Sid were all Australian champions.

Obviously the influence of the Cavill side of the family came through to Eve but the fact that his father was the manager of the Manly Baths must have assisted his swimming development.

Dick Eve went to the 1924 Games where he entered all three diving events. In the high dive-ordinary, or plain dive, there were twenty-five competitors. Going into the final he needed a good performance to win as the Swede, Jansson, was leading.

Eve's last dive was magnificent. He performed the swallow dive and it was judged a perfect performance. He ended up winning the competition from Jansson.

Dick Eve suffered from ear trouble throughout most of his career and this was the case at the Olympics. Nevertheless he competed in the two other events but failed to win another medal.

Richmond Eve was a part of the 'Manly Connection' at the 1924 Olympics. At those games, Australia won three gold medals and all were won by residents of Manly.

THE NEMETHS OF HUNGARY

There are many famous family connections in Olympic history. In Australia we have the Anderson brothers in yachting, John and Ilsa Konrads of swimming fame, and of course, the Roycroft dynasty in the equestrian.

But the Nemeths of Hungary remain one of the most remarkable in the modern Olympic period!

Imre Nemeth competed at the London Games of 1948 where he won the gold medal for the hammer throw. He was a small man, as far as throwers go, weighing only 83 kilograms.

Imre's son, Miklos, was two years old when his father achieved his Olympic victory. As he grew up he was guided towards the athletic field but rather than following his father's footsteps by taking up the hammer, he turned his attention to the javelin.

By the time the 1968 Mexico City Olympics came around, Miklos was ranked second in the world but unfortunately, due to an elbow injury, he failed to gain a medal. In 1972 at Munich he again was one of the favourites, but this time finished a disappointing seventh.

The pressure of being the son of an Olympic champion was telling.

Finally, at the age of twenty-nine, he faced up to his third Olympiad in Montreal. He was no longer a favourite but he was determined to make his mark in the history of his chosen discipline.

Nemeth put everything into his first throw. He raced down the track and as he reached the throwing mark, he launched his javelin with such extraordinary power that he set a new world record. The distance was 94.58 metres which was three metres further than he had ever thrown before. Miklos Nemeth had finally emulated his father's feat of winning an Olympic gold medal.

Imre and Miklos Nemeth remain the only father and son combination ever to win track and field gold medals in Olympic competition.

The final of the men's hockey at the 1972 Munich Olympics between Germany and Pakistan was a bitter and violent contest. Michael Krause of Germany scored the only goal with ten minutes to play. The Pakistani team and their supporters were so furious at the officiating that they stormed the judges' table and poured water over the president of the International Hockey Federation. At the medal ceremony, several Pakistani players refused to face the German flag during the playing of the German national anthem. All eleven Pakistani players were banned for life by the IOC although reinstated in time for the next Olympics.

GOLD, GOLD, GOLD

The men's medley relay final at the Moscow Olympics of 1980 produced one of the most famous race descriptions ever heard on Australian radio.

Due to the Afghanistan invasion by the Soviet Union, the United States boycotted the Moscow games and everyone believed the swimming events would be dominated by the Russians and their Eastern bloc neighbours.

A medley relay team comprises four swimmers all of whom swim a different stroke—backstroke, breaststroke, butterfly and freestyle. Of the competitors in the 1980 final, the Soviet swimmers all had swum faster times than the Australians in each of the individual events and were considered the favourites.

Mark Kerry led off for Australia in the backstroke leg and was fourth at the changeover point. Peter Evans was next, swimming breaststroke, and he managed to maintain fourth position. Mark Tonelli followed with butterfly and he made up precious ground on his Russian counterpart. However when Neil Brooks hit the water for the freestyle leg, he was still almost three metres behind the Soviet, Kopiakov.

Brooks swam the race of his life. He chased his rival down the first lap and with ten metres to go in the race, he had drawn level. The West Australian then took a deep breath and powered his way to the wall and touched first.

As the ABC's Norman May shouted down the microphone, 'It's gold to Australia, ... gold, gold.'

> The Australian sectional manager for boxing at the Melbourne Games, Bill McAuliffe, died during those Games. The same fate happened to Jim Howlin, the sectional manager for athletics in Mexico City (1968).

WATER POLO WAR

In early November 1956, some 200,000 Soviet troops invaded Hungary to quash a major revolt against communist rule. This incident led to a number of countries boycotting the Melbourne Olympics.

As the water polo competition reached its final stages, it soon became clear Hungary would play the USSR in a semi-final.

When the game was held, it became nothing more than a brawl.

Throughout the match, players from both sides exchanged kicks and punches and the referee ordered five participants out of the water. Then a Soviet player punched a Hungarian in the eye while the ball was at the other end of the pool. The water ran red with blood.

Hungarian officials and spectators alike jumped the barriers and confronted the Soviets by yelling and shaking their fists at them. Only the involvement of police prevented a riot. The match was halted by the referee with Hungary leading 4–0 and they were credited with a victory.

Hungary went on to beat Yugoslavia for the gold medal, making it their fourth gold in five Olympics.

Following the Melbourne Games, half the Hungarian delegation refused to return to their homeland and many eventually ended up settling in Australia.

> Would you believe there was a false start for the marathon at the 1956 Games in Melbourne. Following the re-start, the event was won by Frenchman Alain Mimoun. Mimoun was wearing his lucky number thirteen.

WILLIAM TELL OF THE SOLOMONS

In 1987, as part of an Olympic solidarity project, two officials from Archery Australia went off to the Solomon Islands to introduce Olympic-style archery to the locals. When the officials' archery equipment did not arrive, they had to improvise with native bows and arrows. While the locals were most enthusiastic about this new sport, the officials believed it would be some time before they would field an archer in Olympic competition.

The following year, at the Seoul Games, Keith Gaisford, one of the original officials who had travelled to the Solomons, was surprised to find Derek Tenai at the Olympics representing his native country. Gaisford was further surprised to learn Tenai only had a beginner's bow and aluminium arrows.

Arrangements were made to equip Tenai with a state-of-the-art bow as well as a sight, quiver, arm guard and the newest carbon arrows.

During the official practice day, Tenai managed to wipe out several of these arrows but eventually got the hang of his new equipment and prepared to take his place in the Olympic competition.

Derek Tenai did not have a very good meet, in terms of results, in fact he finished dead last, however he impressed many who came in contact with him at Seoul. He seemed to be beaming every day as he left the firing line and he had a wonderful time while facing the best in the world.

Derek Tenai did set one record in Seoul. He became the first Solomon Islander to take part in an Olympic archery competition and no-one can take this honour away from him.

BABE DIDRIKSON

Mildred 'Babe' Didrikson, who was born in Texas of Norwegian parents, is often credited with being the greatest all-round female athlete in history.

At the 1932 US national athletic championships, Didrikson was the only representative of her club. She won five events and single-handedly won the national club competition. The team that came second to her fielded twenty-two athletes.

Following this performance the 18-year-old was selected to compete at the Los Angeles Olympic Games in three events. Rules prohibited her from entering more events. She won the 80-metre hurdles and the javelin, both with world-record performances.

In her third event, the high jump, Babe again broke the world record but was only awarded the silver medal. The judges ruled that she had dived over the bar and in 1932, this particular style of jumping was judged to be illegal. Had she been jumping today this amazing athlete would have been given the green light and pocketed another gold medal.

In her early career Babe Didrikson had been an All-American softball and basketball player and following her Olympic performances at Los Angeles, she turned her hand to golf and dominated the professional ranks.

Babe married well-known wrestler George Zaharias and died of cancer at the very early age of 42.

In the 1980s a poll was taken among American sports editors and journalists to determine the greatest-ever female athlete in the world. Finalists included Chris Evert, Billie Jean King and Wilma Rudolph... but the winner was Babe Didrikson.

> Between 1896 and 1968, the United States took out every pole vault competition in the Olympics. This is the longest streak of victories in Games history.

IAN O'BRIEN

Ian O'Brien was born in the central NSW farming community of Wellington in 1947. He was a strong, well-built youngster and by the time he was fourteen, was a schoolboy swimming sensation in his chosen discipline of breaststroke.

When O'Brien came to the 'big smoke' of Sydney he naturally gravitated to ex-world record holder and fellow breaststroker, Terry Gathercole. Gathercole was himself a bushie having grown up and done most of his swimming in West Wyalong and was now making his mark as a successful coach.

In 1962 O'Brien won his first national title and later that year he went on to participate in the Commonwealth Games in Perth. His first foray into international competition proved most successful as he finished these games with a collection of three gold medals.

But the Olympics are the big one and along with coach Gathercole, O'Brien set his sights on the 200-metre breaststroke event at the Tokyo Games in 1964.

O'Brien won his heat, however several other contenders also made their mark. One was the USA's great Chet Jastremski who had dominated breaststroke swimming over the previous four years, and the other was the current world record holder, Russian Georgy Prokopenko. All three swimmers made it through the semi-finals and going into the final it was a classic case of the underdog nation of Australia, taking on the superpowers of America and the USSR.

Jastremski took off fast and Prokopenko followed. By the 150-metre mark the Aussie had passed Chet the Jet and in an exciting finish, he caught and passed the Russian. At the age of seventeen, Ian O'Brien became an Olympic champion. His time of

2 minutes 27.8 seconds was not only an Olympic record, it also established a new world mark. The boy from Wellington also gained a bronze medal in Tokyo in the Australian medley relay team.

Ian O'Brien's career continued until 1968. While he managed to win another two gold medals at the Jamaican Commonwealth Games of 1966, he failed to repeat his Tokyo performance at the Mexico City Olympics.

At the Barcelona Games of 1992 the Spanish soccer team made it through to the final without giving up a single goal. Their shut-out record came to a prompt end when Poland's Wojciech Kowalczyk put one past their goalie at the end of the first half. The Poles were still ahead well into the second period and it wasn't until the arrival of King Juan Carlos that the Spanish team picked up their game and went on to take out the gold medal.

THE PEARCE FAMILIES

There are two Pearce families who have left their mark on Australian Olympic history.

The Pearce brothers of Perth are considered to be amongst the greats of Australian hockey. Eric, Julian, Gordon and Mel have all played for Australia at the Olympic Games while a fifth brother, Cec, has also represented Australia in international competition.

Eric, Gordon and Mel were members of Australia's first Olympic hockey team in 1956 and twelve years later, at Mexico City, Eric and Gordon won a silver medal. Julian played in the side at the 1964 Tokyo Games.

The other Pearce family were rowers. Bobby Pearce was perhaps the greatest rower the world has ever seen. He won the Olympic single sculls title at consecutive Games, 1928 and 1932. Bobby's cousin Cecil rowed in the single sculls at the Berlin Games of 1936. Cec's son Gary was a member of the eights that won a silver medal in Mexico City.

There are several other well-known Australian Olympic families. John and Ilsa Konrads represented the nation in swimming during the 1960s. Bill Roycroft and his sons Wayne, Clarke and Barry all participated in equestrian events at different Olympics. And the Anderson twins, John and Tom, won gold medals in separate yachting events on the same day at the 1972 Munich Games.

> When the Soviet Union beat Yugoslavia 1–0 in the final of the Olympic soccer tournament on 8 December in 1956, they went into the history books as the winners of the latest gold medal ever won in an Olympic year.

GAIL NEALL

Gail Neall's victory in the 400-metre individual medley at the Munich Olympics of 1972 exemplified the saying, 'Getting it right on the day'.

Coming into the Games, Neall was not nearly as well known as her schoolmate from Turramurra High, Shane Gould. Shane had captured all the headlines and the whole of Australia was focused on what this multi-talented swimmer might do.

Yet it was Neall who delivered the most pleasant of surprises! Gail had swum in the heats of the 200-metre individual medley but failed to progress any further. In the 200-metre butterfly she made it through to the final but could only manage a seventh placing. But after getting through to the last eight of the 400-metre individual medley she prepared herself for the swim of her life.

Swimming in lane seven, the seventeen-year-old started well and found herself leading at the end of the butterfly leg. She continued to hold this lead throughout the backstroke leg and even at the end of the breaststroke, her weakest stroke, Neall was still ahead.

Finally, during the first lap of freestyle the pace began to tell. Neall was overtaken by the Canadian Leslie Cliff and with 50 metres remaining in the race it seemed as though her dreams of Olympic glory were dashed. But this shy youngster, whose only previous international experience had been at the 1970 Commonwealth Games, called on all her reserves to produce an amazing performance. She regained the lead and managed to beat the Canadian by less than a second. Her time of 5 minutes 02.97 seconds was both an Olympic and world record.

For her amazing swim at Munich, Gail Neall was honoured by the Helms Foundation. She was awarded their most prestigious trophy as Australasia's outstanding athlete for 1972.

SOCCER TURMOIL IN 1936

At the 1936 Berlin Olympic Games during the Soccer quarter-final between Peru and Austria, the score was level when Peruvian fans rushed onto the field and attacked one of the Austrian players.

The Peruvian team took advantage of the chaos to score two quick goals and win 4–2.

Austria protested and the International Jury of Appeal ordered a replay two days' later declaring the match had to be played behind closed doors, with no spectators.

The Peruvians refused to show up and the entire Peruvian contingent withdrew from the Games as did the Colombians in support of their South American neighbour.

The first brother and sister to represent Australia at an Olympic Games were Frank and Lily Beaurepaire. The year was 1920 and the Games were in Antwerp. Frank came away from those Games with a silver medal in the freestyle relay and a bronze in the 1500 metres. Lily, while competing in three swimming races as well as a diving competition, failed to secure a placing.

BOYCOTTS

Boycotts have been the scourge of the modern Olympic movement.

In 1956 several countries refused to attend the Games due to tension existing in various hot spots around the world. Russia had quelled a Hungarian uprising and British involvement with the Suez Canal caused nations like Egypt, Lebanon, Switzerland and the Netherlands not to show up in Melbourne.

In 1976 the Olympics were again used for political gain. New Zealand's rugby team were playing in South Africa and many African countries demanded they withdraw from the tour. When they refused, officials led some 440 athletes out of Montreal. Magnificent runners such as Filbert Bayi, John Akii Bua and Mike Boit were denied the right to line up for Olympic gold.

When the Soviet Union invaded Afghanistan, America refused to compete at the 1980 Moscow Games. Australia was dragged into the conflict when Prime Minister Malcolm Fraser applied pressure to the Australian Olympic Federation to follow suit. The AOF refused and voted 6–5 to send a team.

The Los Angeles Games of 1984 were hit by a Soviet-led boycott for what had happened in 1980. No event was harder hit than the freestyle wrestling discipline. Twenty-three of the thirty medallists from the previous year's world championships were from boycotting nations including nine of the ten gold medallists. The light-flyweight division was so depleted that there were only seven entrants—the smallest wrestling competition in more than fifty years.

> In the 1906 Athens Games, there was an event in fencing for the three-corned sabre. It was won by Gustav Casmir of Germany. This was the one and only time this event was included in Olympic competition.

THE STOCKHOLM OLYMPIC GAMES OF 1912

The first four modern Olympic Games struggled to make their mark as great sporting festivals. Athens had been a mere gathering of some three hundred athletes. The Paris Games, in 1900, went for a period of five months and was nothing like the spectacle we know today. St Louis was an extension of the United States celebration of the Louisiana Purchase. And London, while being well organised, became somewhat restrictive with entries only being accepted by way of individual Olympic committees.

It was the Stockholm Games of 1912 which firmly re-established the Olympic movement and rekindled the spirit which had existed in ancient times.

There were twenty-eight nations represented in the Swedish capital and just over 2500 athletes took part in these Games. Australasia sent a team of twenty-five competitors including three from New Zealand.

All medals won by Australians in 1912 were in the swimming pool. Sarah 'Fanny' Durack was our only individual gold medallist winning the first ever 100-metre freestyle event for women. Her compatriot Mina Wylie took out the silver in this same event.

Our 4 x 200-metres freestyle relay was also successful in winning and a member of that team, Cecil Healy, picked up the silver in the men's 100-metre freestyle. Harold Hardwick collected two individual bronze medals for the 400-metre and 1500-metre freestyle.

Several notable individuals competed at the Stockholm Games. George Smith Patton Jnr, later known to the world as American General Patton, was a competitor in the first modern pentathlon and finished fifth. Another American in that same event was Avery Brundage who was later to become the president of the International Olympic Committee.

Also taking part in these Games was an American Indian by the name of Jim Thorpe. Thorpe won both the decathlon and pentathlon and many consider him to be the greatest all-round athlete the world has ever seen.

The father of surfboard riding in Australia, Hawaiian Duke Kahanamoku, won the 100-metre freestyle and repeated his victory at Antwerp in 1920.

Australia has competed at every Games of the modern era and on only four occasions has failed to pick up gold. The last time was in Montreal (1976). At those Games our athletes came home with one silver and four bronze medals. After our 'disastrous' showing in Canada, the Federal Government was spurred on to establish the Institute of Sport in Canberra.

WOMEN WIN HOCKEY GOLD IN 1988

The Australian men's hockey team first played in an Olympic tournament when the Games were held in Melbourne in 1956. Since then, they have established themselves as one of the strongest hockey-playing nations in the world but have never managed to win the elusive gold medal.

In 1968 at Mexico City, the Aussie men made it through to the Olympic final only to be defeated by Pakistan. Again in Montreal (1976) they played in the final but this time they went down to our cousins from across the Tasman, the New Zealanders.

By the time Seoul came around they were again looking to the gold medal but this time only managed a fourth.

At these same Games, Australia's women's team were competing in their second Olympics yet they were able to perform on the world hockey stage with much gusto.

The major highlight in their campaign came when they beat the powerful Netherlands team, 3–2, in the semi-final. This loss ended a decade of domination of women's hockey by the Dutch and set up a final against the host nation, South Korea.

While this match was somewhat anti-climactic, the agile Koreans, playing before a partisan crowd of 26,000 fanatical supporters, kept the Aussie women on their toes. Finally, goals by captain Debbie Bowman and Lee Capes captured the game and Australia won its first gold in a sport it had been endeavouring to conquer for so many years.

> When the Australian swim team of thirty-two headed off to Rome in 1960, eight of its members held, between them, twenty-five world records.

NEW ZEALAND'S PETER SNELL

Over the years, New Zealand has produced many Olympic champions in the middle- and long-distance events on the track. In 1936, Jack Lovelock was successful in knocking off the best in the world in the 1500 metres at the Berlin Games. At Rome it was Murray Halberg who won the 5000 metres. And in the 1970s John Walker reigned supreme over the mile and 1500 metres.

But none was more famous than Peter Snell. Snell was born at Opunake and as a schoolboy was a superb athlete. He set Auckland junior cross-country records when he was thirteen and ran the mile in 4 minutes 48.4 seconds when he was only fifteen. In 1958 he came under the tutorage of Arthur Lydiard, the doyen of New Zealand track and field coaches.

Lydiard nurtured Snell and in March 1960 he sent his pupil to Australia to race against the famous Herb Elliott. Snell beat Elliott over 880 yards, one of the few times Elliott was defeated in his career. This victory gained him a place on the NZ Olympic team to Rome.

In Rome, Lydiard set his charge the task of beating the Belgian, Moens, in the 800 metres. Snell made it through to the final and after a tactical race, he found he was running second to Moens with only the final straight to go. The New Zealander gave it everything he had and took the lead twenty metres from the tape. He hung on, causing the upset of the Games and winning his first gold medal.

Four years later in Tokyo, Peter Snell had prepared himself for the glamour 1500 metre event. However, he was running so well he decided to take on both the 1500 and the 800 metres.

Over the shorter distance Snell easily qualified for the final but at the bell lap he found he was boxed in. He dropped back, swung wide and unleashed a burst which took him past the field and enabled him to win by four metres.

In the 1500 metres Snell was again boxed in with a lap to go but this time a British runner moved inside to let him through to third position on the curve. He made the most of the opportunity and turned on one of the finest finishes in Olympic history. Peter Snell won his third gold medal and established his mark on Olympic history.

The 1948 Olympic basketball tournament had some unusual highlights. A British referee was knocked unconscious during a preliminary game between Chile and Iraq; a Chinese player dribbled between the legs of the US centre, Bob Kurland, and followed through to score a basket; the Iraqi team twice lost by 100 points; Ireland's offensive was equally as poor averaging only 17 points a game; and in the fiercely contested match for third place, a Brazilian player lost his pants and had to retire to the dressing room. Meanwhile, the US beat France 65–21 in a lopsided final.

JON HENRICKS

Australia's Jon Henricks was the winner of the prestigious 100-metre freestyle event at the Melbourne Olympics. He won a second gold medal as a member of the 4 x 200-metre relay team.

But Henricks left his mark on swimming for another reason. At the 1953 NSW state championships it was Henricks who became the first swimmer to shave his body before competing in a big meet.

The Henricks family lived on the Parramatta River and Jon's father had observed the preparations the yachting fraternity undertook before competing in a regatta. He noticed the crews spent a lot of time cleaning and polishing the hulls of their boats so as to allow them to slip through the water faster.

Henricks Snr. convinced his son he should emulate this by shaving his body.

This practice is now accepted as the norm. It prevents drag and has proved to be one of the greatest innovations in swimming over the past fifty years.

A little-known fact about our first Olympian and dual gold medallist Edwin Flack is that he competed in both the singles and doubles of tennis in Athens (1896). His partner in the doubles was an Englishman called Robertson and they were eliminated in the first round. During the day when the victory ceremonies were held, Robertson, who was a professor at Oxford University, recited an Olympic Ode which he had composed.

FIRST OLYMPIC GOLD WALKOVER

At the 1908 Olympics held in London, all the officials who adjudicated in the various competitions came from the host country. At times, their judgments were deemed as anti-American, especially by members of the USA press.

The most controversial incident occurred in the 400-metre track event which was not run in lanes.

Three Americans and one Englishman were entered in the race which was easily won by J.C. Carpenter of the USA. However, the British officials claimed he had fouled the English runner Wyndham Halswelle, and disqualified him.

A re-run of the event was ordered but the American contingent refused to take part.

Hence Halswelle won in what was to become the first Olympic Games' walkover.

At the Olympic Games of 1964 in Tokyo, Great Britain won its first-ever gold medals in women's events at track and field. Mary Rand won the long jump with a new world record, and Ann Packer took out the 800-metre event. They were room-mates in the Olympic village.

FORGOTTEN HEROES

Australia had many wonderful victories the last time the Olympic Games were held in Australia. The names of Betty Cuthbert, Dawn Fraser and Murray Rose have gone down in sporting history following their successes at Melbourne in 1956.

However, there were several other 'golden heroes' from those games.

In the 4 x 100-metre relay on the track Betty Cuthbert and Shirley Strickland, both individual gold medallists, were ably supported by Norma Croker and Fleur Mellor to win that event.

And in the swimming pool, the great Dawn Fraser and Lorraine Crapp were assisted by the likes of Faith Leech and Sandra Morgan to gain success in the 4 x 100-metre freestyle relay. With Morgan's gold came the honour of being Australia's youngest Olympic gold medallist. She was fourteen years of age.

Kevin O'Halloran is another unsung hero. This unlikely gold medallist came from rural Western Australia and was a member of Australia's triumphant 4 x 200-metre relay. His accomplishment is perhaps overshadowed by his fellow team-mates, Murray Rose, John Devitt and Jon Henricks. All these swimmers won individual gold medals.

Two other Australians who won gold in Melbourne were Ian Browne and Tony Marchant. These two cyclists paired up to take out the 2000-metre tandem, an event which is rarely contested these days.

> The Soviet Union first sent athletes to an Olympic Games in 1952. Perhaps it was because the Games in that year were held in a neighbouring country, Finland.

BRAD COOPER

It was at the Munich Olympic Games, in 1972, that the great Shane Gould etched her mark into Australian sporting history. She won three gold medals, a silver and a bronze.

There were other wonderful Australian swimming performances at those Games. Gail Neall was a surprise winner in the 200-metre individual medley and Bev Whitfield defeated Russia's Galina Stepanova in the 200-metre breaststroke.

But another Australian took gold in the pool. His name is Brad Cooper and he is the proud owner of a gold medal for the 400-metre freestyle.

Cooper finished second to the American Rick de Mont and was defeated by the barest of margins, one hundredth of a second. He was presented with his silver medal and he thought that was that.

The next day it was announced there was a problem with de Mont's drug test and he was found positive for taking the banned pill ephedrine. He was stripped of the Olympic crown and this immediately caused a problem. One senior IOC member wanted the title to remain vacant, with no gold medal being awarded. The Australian Chef de Mission, Julius Patching appealed to the IOC president and it was decided to give Cooper the gold.

De Mont believed he was the legitimate owner of the medal and he took off to the States with the one he received at the presentation ceremony. It was not until the evening before the Australian team were due to leave Munich that Cooper received his gold medal.

Much of the Brad Cooper story has been overshadowed by the other Australian swimmers at the 1972 Games but it should be remembered that he too, is also an Olympic champion and gold medallist.

FIRST WOMEN'S MARATHON

The first women's marathon to be held at the Olympic Games took place in Los Angeles in 1984.

Women had been pushing for the inclusion of the marathon in the Olympic program for years. It had been internationally competed by females for some two decades, however officials from the International Olympic Committee believed that such a distance was too demanding for women.

Fifty-one competitors entered the first women's Olympic marathon. Prerace favourites were American Joan Benoit and Norwegian Grete Waitz and they ended up finishing first and second. Benoit's time was 2 hours 24 minutes and 52 seconds. Australia's Lisa Martin was regarded as a strong medal prospect going into the Games but came in seventh in a time of 2 hours 29 minutes and 3 seconds.

Germany's Steffi Graf won the singles title in the 1988 Olympic demonstration sport of tennis when she was fifteen years of age. Just one week before the Games began, Graf had become only the fifth player in history to win a tennis Grand Slam.

ROMANIA'S LIA MANOLIU

Discus thrower Lia Manoliu from Romania holds two Olympic records which may never be broken. Not only is she the oldest woman in Olympic history to win a gold medal, but she competed in six consecutive Games. No other female track and field athlete has taken part in this many competitions.

Manoliu started her Olympic quest at Helsinki in 1952. At those Games she finished sixth. Four years later, in Melbourne, she placed ninth and in Rome she got amongst the medals with a bronze. At the Tokyo Games she came up against the USSR's Tamara Press, one of the famous Press sisters, and once again could only manage a third placing.

It was at Mexico in 1968 that she finally succeeded. Going into the event Manoliu was suffering an elbow injury. She decided to put everything into her first throw and hurled the discus 58.28 metres. This was well short of the world record of 62.54 metres held by Liesel Westermann of Germany, but good enough to lead the competition. Then the Romanian fouled three times, passed once, and got off a poor throw with her last effort.

A rainstorm had arrived during the second round and all the competitors were severely hampered in the throwing circle as the conditions became wetter and wetter. In the end Lia Manoliu's effort in the first round was good enough to take out first place and the 36-year-old became the oldest female track and field gold medallist.

Manoliu went to Munich in 1972 but could only manage a ninth place finish. However by taking part in her sixth Olympics she carved her name into Olympic history.

> The President of the United States Olympic Committee at the time of the Amsterdam Games in 1928 was General of the Army, Douglas MacArthur.

DECATHLON'S GREATEST COMPETITION

The decathlon is considered the most gruelling of athletic competitions. It consists of ten different events and takes place over two days. In 1960 at the Rome Olympic Games, perhaps the greatest decathlon competition of all time took place in the Stadio Olympico. The two main players were Rafer Johnson of the USA and C.K. Yang of Taiwan.

Both Johnson and Yang had competed at the Melbourne Olympics. The American had finished second and Yang was eighth. By the time Rome came around, the two rivals were great friends and team-mates attending university together at UCLA.

The first day of competition was interrupted by a thunderstorm and did not end until 11 p.m. After the first five events Johnson led Yang by a mere 55 points.

The combatants were back at the track the next morning at 9 a.m. The first event was the 110-metre hurdles and Johnson failed to score anywhere near his best. He hit a hurdle and ran a slow 15.9 seconds. Yang picked up valuable points. The day progressed and going into the last event, the 1500 metres, the American led by 67 points.

The four-lap race was a battle supreme. It started at 9.15 p.m. and Yang, the better middle distance runner, set off like a hare. Johnson hung on and over the last 400 metres, the Taiwanese tried to shake his friend. It did not happen. Johnson finished only six metres behind Yang and managed to take the gold medal. It had been a Herculean struggle. The Italian crowd appreciated what they had witnessed over the two days and rose, en masse, to applaud these two great athletes.

Yang, while missing the ultimate prize, took out Taiwan's first

Olympic medal and became a hero back in his country.

Rafer Johnson became an actor and in 1968 was again thrust onto the world stage. When Senator Robert Kennedy was shot and killed in a Los Angeles hotel, it was Johnson who struggled and caught the assassin. In 1984 he was given the honour of lighting the torch at the Opening Ceremony of the Los Angeles Olympics.

Cuba completly dominated the boxing competition at the Barcelona Games in 1992. Out of the twelve gold medals given in this sport, athletes from this small Caribbean country won seven. They also took out two silver medals. This was the best performance by any nation in a nonboycotted Olympics.

FENCING MASTER

One of the most amazing performances in Olympic history took place at the Antwerp Games of 1920 by Italian fencing master Nedo Nadi.

Nadi attended his first Games in Stockholm in 1912 when he was only eighteen years old, a very young age for a fencer. Yet he came away the victor in the individual foil event and won his first gold medal.

The Games were not held in 1916 due to World War I and by the time Antwerp came around Nadi was a true fencing supremo. The performance he turned in at those Games was nothing short of sensational. The Italian won an unprecedented five gold medals. Not only was he the champion in both the individual foil and sabre titles, but he also led the Italians in the foil, épée and sabre teams events.

With the five gold medals he won in Antwerp and the one he obtained eight years previously, Nedo Nadi stamped himself as one of the all-time great Olympic champions.

Federico (Fritz) Dennerlein was a member of the Italian water polo team which placed fourth at the Melbourne Olympics. Fritz was also a very good butterfly swimmer and four years later in Rome, he decided to pass up his chance to be on the water polo team and concentrate on the 200-metre 'fly event. In the final, Fritz placed fourth. The Italian team took out the gold in water polo.

TEAM HANDBALL

It may come as a surprise to many Australians but the sport of handball has been on the Olympic program since 1936. But don't confuse it with the game we play here. It bears no similarity.

Olympic handball, or as it is officially known, team handball, is a fast and exciting sport. It is perhaps best described as a cross between basketball and soccer. The ball is moved around the 40 metre by 20 metre court by passing and dribbling. However instead of shooting it into a basket, it is thrown past a goalie and into a goal.

There are seven players on a team. Apart from the goalie, there are big shooters, middle backcourt players, wings and circle players.

A player may take three steps before and after dribbling but he or she may not hold the ball for more than three seconds without dribbling or passing.

Games are divided into two thirty-minute halves. In preliminary matches, ties are allowed to stand but in semi-finals and finals overtime is played.

The European countries are the dominant powers in team handball but Australia, as the host nation in 2000, will definitely have a team in the competition. Hence, if there are any young Australians out there who are looking for a new and different sport which they might like to take up with dreams of Olympic participation, team handball might be the way to go!

> In 1920, France's Suzanne Lenglen introduced short skirts as the uniform for the Olympic tennis tournament. Lenglen won a gold medal as a member of the mixed doubles team and a bronze in the doubles.

BUSTER CRABBE

Between 1924 and 1932 three names dominated the world of swimming. One was the celebrated Johnny Weissmuller who won back-to-back Olympic titles in the 100-metre freestyle and went on to become the most famous of Tarzans on the movie screen.

The second big name was Australia's Andrew 'Boy' Charlton. Charlton was the Olympic champion for 1500 metres at the Paris Games of 1924 and he continued to swim through until 1932 and had several other placings in this highest form of athletic competition.

The third person who was at the forefront of aquatic endeavour was Sweden's Arne Borg. Borg's swims against Charlton are legendary. When he faced up to Charlton in a race at the old Domain pool in Sydney, it is reported over 50,000 people witnessed the event.

But there was a fourth great of world swimming at this time of which little is ever written. His name was Clarence 'Buster' Crabbe.

Crabbe had successes at two Olympics. At Amsterdam in 1928 he was up against both Charlton and Borg and he managed to come a creditable third in the 1500 metres. In the 400 metres he finished fourth behind the winner Zorrilla of Argentina and Charlton and Borg. His time was less than four seconds behind Zorrilla and in that era this was considered a close finish.

Four years later Crabbe again swam the double. This time he could only manage fifth in the 1500 metres but he took out the gold medal in the 400 metres. The race was led by Jean Taris of France for most of the distance. It was only in the last 25 metres that Crabbe drew even with the world-record holder. The excitement of the crowd was electrifying. People rushed to view the end of the race and Weissmuller, who had been sitting in the front row, jumped the fence to gain a better vantage point.

Crabbe won by inches and he is quoted as saying, 'That one-tenth of a second changed my life.' The reason why? Crabbe came to the attention of Hollywood producers and went on to become famous as a movie star.

Buster Crabbe is not known to the world as an Olympic champion but rather for his roles as Tarzan, Buck Rogers and Flash Gordon.

> At each Opening Ceremony an athlete from the host country makes the following oath on behalf of all athletes: 'In the name of all competitors, I promise that we shall take part in these Olympic Games, respecting and abiding by the rules which govern them, in the true spirit of sportsmanship for the glory of sport and the honour of our teams.'

ODDJOB

The winner of the gold medal in the weightlifting light heavyweight division at the 1948 London Olympic Games was Stanley Stanczyk. The American won over the audience not only because of his superior lifting—he won by a margin of 37.5 kg—but because of his outstanding sportsmanship.

With his third snatch he attempted a new world record. He hoisted the weight and the judges signalled a fair lift. However Stanczyk shook his head and tapped his leg indicating his knee had scraped the floor. This action invalidated the lift and denied him the record.

Also lifting in this competition was another American, Harold Sakata. Sakata took out the silver medal and following the Games became a successful professional wrestler using the name Tosh Togo.

But it was neither as a weightlifter nor as a wrestler that Sakata achieved fame.

He turned his hand to acting and eventually reached international stardom in one of the James Bond movies. The film was *Goldfinger* and the character he played was the evil Oddjob.

The Czech Robert Zmelik won the gruelling decathlon at the 1992 Games in Barcelona. Travelling in a taxi shortly after his victory, Zmelik left his precious gold medal in the cab and thought he had lost it forever. Thankfully for Zmelik, the driver was an honest man and the medal was returned.

SAMARANCH

The man who heads up the Olympic movement on the world stage today is Juan Antonio Samaranch.

This high-profile leader was born in 1920 in the Catalonian town of Barcelona, Spain. His interest in sport began when he took up boxing in the early 1940s fighting under the name of Kid Samaranch. As a young man he also played hockey and soccer.

Professionally, Samaranch pursued a career in economics and served on the board of several banks. He was a municipal councillor responsible for sport in the city of Barcelona. Later on he served as ambassador to the USSR and also to the People's Republic of Mongolia.

Samaranch has had a distinguished career in international sports administration. He was Spain's Chef de Mission at the Rome and Tokyo Olympics and was made a member of the IOC in 1966. In 1980 he was made president of this most august body.

Samaranch is fluent in Spanish, French and English and has some knowledge of Russian and German. He also has a keen interest in stamp collecting.

The original Mean Machine in swimming was not the medley relay team that won gold in 1980 but rather the 4 x 100-metre freestyle relay team at the Commonwealth Games in Brisbane two years later. The medley relay team is often referred to as the GOLD, GOLD, GOLD team. This is in line with the famous call by radio commentator Norman May.

OLYMPIAD

The term 'Olympiad' is defined as a four-year period beginning with the opening of the Games of a particular Olympiad and ending on the opening of the Games of the following Olympiad.

The widely used terms 'Summer Olympics' and 'Winter Olympics' are technically incorrect. The 'Games of the Olympiad' refers to the Games held during the summer every four years, and the 'Olympic Winter Games', while initially held in the same calendar year as the Olympic Games, are now held two years afterwards.

The Winter Games were held in Lillehammer, Norway in 1994, in Nagano, Japan in 1998 and will be held in 2002 in Salt Lake City, USA.

The Games of the first modern Olympiad were held in Athens, Greece in 1896 and every Olympiad is numbered consecutively from that year.

In 2000, the Games of the twenty-seventh Olympiad will be held in Sydney.

German diver Ingrid Kramer has the distinction of competing at three different Olympics under three different names. In 1960, as Kramer, she won both the highboard and springboard titles. Four years later in Tokyo, she captured a gold and a silver under the name Ingrid Engel and at Mexico City she was known as Ingrid Gilbin.

1500-METRE WALK

The 1500 metre walking event has been held only once in Olympic competition—at the Intercalated or Interim Games of 1906. These Games were held in Athens on the tenth anniversary of the first modern Games and this particular event, the walk, caused quite a stir.

The first two competitors to cross the line were disqualified. Richard Wilkinson from Britain and Austria's Eugen Spiegler were 'outed' for illegal technique. This left George Bonhag of the USA as the winner.

However two of the four judges also thought Bonhag should be disqualified. They claimed he, too, did not walk 'correctly'. It was left up to the president of the jury to cast a deciding vote and he voted in favour of the American.

Interestingly, Bonhag had never previously entered a walking race. At these Games he had competed in the 5-mile run and the 1500-metre run but was disappointed with both showings. He had finished fourth and sixth respectively. He thus entered the walk and became an Olympic champion at his first attempt at the discipline.

A Greek, Charilaos Vasilakos, placed fifth in this walking race and ten years' earlier, at the first Olympics, had placed second in the marathon. You had to be versatile at the turn of the century!

The man who came within a whisker of defeating Cassius Clay (Muhammad Ali) at the 1960 Olympic Games in Rome was an Australian. His name was Tony Madigan and he fought Clay in the semi-final of the light heavyweight division.

GOLDS FOR TWO DIFFERENT COUNTRIES

One of the more interesting facts about Australia's history at the Olympic Games is that in 1908 they were successful in winning the gold medal—for rugby. This was Australia's only gold at the London Games.

A member of that victorious Wallaby team was Daniel Carroll.

Rugby competition was not held in 1912 and the Games of 1916 were cancelled due to World War I. When the Olympics resumed, at Antwerp in 1920, rugby was once again on the program.

This time the gold medal was won by the Americans when they defeated France 8–0. But playing in the US team was one Daniel Carroll. It is recorded that Daniel Carroll is the only person in any sport to win gold medals representing different countries.

At the Seoul Games of 1988, Australia's Grant Davies had his name flashed up on the scoreboard as the winner of the kayak singles event in canoeing. But his jubilation was short lived. The jury of the International Canoe Federation examined the photo-finish picture and declared Davis' rival, Greg Barton from the USA, had won the race by .005 of a second. This time equates to less than 1 centimetre.

RUSSIA'S IVANOV WINS THREE IN A ROW

The red-hot favourite for the single sculls title going into the Melbourne Olympics was Australia's Stuart Mackenzie. The tall, strong, bronzed Aussie, who made his living as a chicken sexer, was leading all the way. Suddenly, with the finish line only 200 metres away, the Russian, Vyacheslav Ivanov, made an incredible spurt and took out the event.

So elated was Ivanov with his victory that upon receiving his gold he jumped up and down with joy and dropped his medal into the depths of Lake Wendouree. He immediately dived into the murky water but came up empty-handed. After the Games were over he was given a replacement medal by the International Olympic Committee.

Vyacheslav Ivanov became something of a legend in rowing circles. In 1960, at Lake Albano, Rome, he defended his Olympic title, this time beating a German by seven seconds. Four years later he again won what many consider the premier event on the Olympic rowing program.

With 500 metres to go he staged another of his famous finishing bursts. He made up eleven seconds on the German Achim Hill, the man he had defeated in Rome.

Years later in his book, *Winds of Olympic Lakes*, Ivanov recalled that he had put such effort into his final burst in Tokyo that he had blacked out before the finish line.

Vyacheslav Ivanov remains the only rower ever to have won the Olympic single sculls title at three consecutive Games. In doing so he places himself in the same category as our own great Dawn Fraser who incidentally won her three golds at the same Games as Ivanov.

MOST GOLD MEDALS

Most people would recognise the name of Mark Spitz. He is the swimmer who won seven gold medals at the Munich Olympic Games in 1972. He also won two golds in Mexico City as a member of two relay teams thus bringing his total golden haul to an incredible nine.

But there are three other individuals who have won nine gold medals in Olympic competition.

The legendary Finnish track runner Paavo Nurmi won a total of nine golds between 1920 and 1928 and Larysa Latynina of the Soviet Union won a similar number between 1956 and 1964. Latynina was a gymnast.

The fourth athlete to accomplish this astonishing feat was Carl Lewis. By winning the long jump at the Atlanta Games Lewis brought his total number of Olympic gold medals to nine.

This victory helped Lewis get into the record books in another category. His fourth consecutive title in the long jump equalled the efforts of Al Oerter and Paul Elvstrom for the number of Most Consecutive Victories in the Same Event. Oerter won the discus throw for the United States from 1956 to 1968 and Elvstrom was a Danish sailor who achieved his successes in the Finn class between 1948 and 1960.

> The Manly Olympic Swimming Pool was renamed the Boy Charlton Pool in 1997 in honour of one of Manly's favourite sons, Andrew 'Boy' Charlton. He was one of Australia's three gold medallists at the 1924 Games and all of them came from the Sydney beachside suburb.

LOVE AT THE OLYMPICS

When so many fit, young athletes from all around the world gather for an Olympic Games, it is only natural that international love matches are spawned. One such affair happened at the Melbourne Games when Harold Connolly of the United States and Olga Fikotova from Czechoslovakia fell in love.

Connolly was the 1956 champion in the hammer throw event and Fikotova won a gold for the discus. Their romance blossomed in the Olympic village in Melbourne, causing great consternation for officials from the Czech Republic. It should be remembered that in those days of the Cold War Czechoslovakia was behind the Iron Curtain.

Finally, after a great deal of pressure, the two were allowed to wed. The marriage took place in Prague and a crowd of over 40,000 was on hand to witness the civil ceremony. The happy couple then settled in the United States.

Connolly attended three more Olympics but could not reach the heights of his Melbourne victory. His wife took part in four more Games, representing the United States, but she too could not repeat her gold of 1956.

Unfortunately their fairytale romance came to an end in 1973 when the pair were divorced.

An interesting footnote to the Fikotova–Connolly story happened in 1972. Prior to the Munich Games of that year Olga was elected by her team-mates to carry the United States flag at the Opening Ceremony. The US Olympic Committee tried to prevent this as the five-time Olympian had been an opponent of US involvement in the Vietnam War. But Olga Connolly was allowed to carry out this honour anyway.

EDWIN FLACK

Edwin Flack was Australia's first Olympic champion. He was twelve months old when his family migrated from England and settled in Melbourne. He was sent to England for two years, in March 1895, to study accountancy and worked for Price, Waterhouse and Co. He took a month's holiday at the time of the 1896 Olympics, travelled from London to Athens as a member of the London Athletic Club, found his own accommodation and took part in the 800 metre and 1500 metre events. The final of the longer event was first and Flack outsprinted the American Arthur Blake in the straight to win by two metres. Two days later he was back on the track for the 800 metre final but in the meantime he had played in the Olympic tennis competition. Flack won the 800 metres with ease. The very next day he ran in the marathon, his first-ever, and led for some time before becoming delirious and retiring.

At the Mexico City Olympics of 1968, only two months following the Soviet occupation of Czechoslovakia, Vera Caslavska won her second gymnastic all-around gold medal in a row. This took her Olympic medal total to seven gold and four silver. The following year, Caslavska became the president of the Czech Olympic Committee.

KLAUS DIBIASI

Italian diver Carlo Dibiasi attended the 1936 Olympic Games in Berlin. While only managing to finish tenth in the platform event he was touched by his Olympic experience and continued to dream of an Olympic gold medal.

Carlo Dibiasi took up coaching and when a son came along he steered him towards the sport at which he represented his country. Young Klaus trained long and hard and most days practised between 130 and 150 dives a day. He did this six days a week.

At the Tokyo Games in 1964 Dibiasi junior picked up a silver medal in platform but four years later he started an incredible run of victories which may never be equalled in the annals of diving.

At Mexico City, Klaus Dibiasi became Italy's first-ever gold medallist in swimming and diving. He won the platform event from a very strong field of Mexicans and Americans. Four years later, at the 1972 Games in Munich, the talented Italian again won the gold, this time from Richard Rydze of the United States.

Montreal, 1976, was to be Klaus Dibiasi's last Olympics and he went out with a blaze of glory. Not only did he win the gold again, he beat a young and talented up-and-coming American-Samoan by the name of Greg Louganis.

Apart from the three golds and a silver in platform diving, Dibiasi also won a silver medal in the springboard event at Mexico City.

> Stylianos Mygiakis from Greece won the featherweight division in Greco-Roman wrestling in 1980. In doing so, he became the first Greek ever to win a Greco-Roman gold medal in Olympic competition.

ROMANIA'S IOLANDA BALAS

Between the mid-1950s and 1966 there was only one person to be considered when it came to the women's high jump. That was Iolanda Balas.

Balas was born in Timisoara, Romania, in 1936. Twenty years later, as the Melbourne Olympic Games approached, she broke the world record, the first of fourteen such records over the next five years.

At the 1956 Olympics Balas could only manage a fifth placing behind the American Mildred McDaniel but after this meet her fortunes changed for the better. In 1958 she took out the European championship and two years later, at Rome, she won her first Olympic crown with a leap of 1.85 metres.

In Tokyo during the first Asian Olympic Games, the Romanian again reigned supreme and this time took out the gold with a height of 1.90 metres.

Iolanda Balas was perhaps the last of the old-fashioned jumpers. She used a version of the 'scissors' jump and found it impossible to adapt to any other style. If she could have adapted, then the world mark she set in 1961 of 1.91 metres could have been raised much higher.

Sydney policeman Peter Macken competed at five Olympic Games in the gruelling sport of modern pentathlon. His first Games were Rome in 1960 and after Montreal he retired.

Unfortunately Macken never won a medal, with his best placing being in Tokyo where he finished fourth.

CARL DIEM

The man who was the custodian of the Olympic movement in Germany during the first three decades of this century was one Carl Diem.

Diem gained his love and enthusiasm for the Olympic ideals when he attended the Interim Games in Athens in 1906. He struck up a friendship with Pierre de Coubertin, the Father of the modern Olympics, and transposed many of the founder's ideas into the German sporting community.

Diem was an outstanding administrator and organiser of sport and led his country's teams to the 1912, 1928 and 1932 Games. It was he who ordered the construction of the stadium in Berlin for the Games of 1916 which never took place. From 1931 on he was General Secretary of the Organising Committee for the 1936 Olympics.

Among his many innovations at the Berlin Games of 1936 was the torch relay. Diem, along with his friend Jean Ketseas, arranged for the flame to be lit in Olympia and carried by relay to the Games city. This feature has remained a part of the Olympic tradition until this day.

Carl Diem lost his influence within Germany with the rise of the Nazis but after de Coubertin's death he continued to produce the Olympic Review.

Olympic youth tours and the founding of the International Olympic Academy can be directly attributed to his vision.

> Great Britain's first Olympic champion was Launceston Elliot. He won his title in the one-hand lift section of the super heavyweight division of weightlifting at the first Games in Athens (1896).

ARTISTIC DISCUS AND SHOT-PUT CHAMPION

Micheline Ostermeyer finished third in the French discus championship of 1948 but this placing gained her a berth on her country's Olympic team to the London Games of that same year.

At those Games Ostermeyer threw the discus more than two feet further than her nearest competitor and took out the coveted gold medal. In doing so she proved to be the most unexpected Olympic champion at the Wembley stadium.

The Frenchwoman also took out the gold in her other throwing event, the shot-put, and placed third in the high jump. A truly versatile athlete.

But her versatility did not confine itself to the athletic field. Ostermeyer was an accomplished musician and was the winner of the Paris Conservatoire piano prize.

Micheline celebrated her Olympic victories in London by giving an impromptu recital of some of Beethoven's most famous works back at her team's headquarters.

The Bahamian boat which finished nineteenth in the Star class at the 1988 Games was skippered by Durwood Knowles who had won this event back in 1964. Knowles was seventy years of age and was the third oldest competitor, in any sport, in the history of the Games. He was competing in his eighth Olympics.

FRANK BEAUREPAIRE

Frank Beaurepaire's swimming career spanned five Olympics. He competed in three, London (1908), Antwerp (1920) and Paris (1924) and while he did not win a gold medal, he did win three silver and three bronze medals. He was denied the chance to compete in 1912 at Stockholm because it was believed that a job he held at the time as a physical education instructor infringed on his amateur status. He was suspended by the International Swimming Federation and later reinstated. Beaurepaire's sister, Lily, also won selection in the 1920 swim team as a sprinter. Together they became the first Australian brother and sister to compete at the Olympics. Sir Frank Beaurepaire later built an empire in car tyres and became Lord Mayor of Melbourne.

The United States men dominated the swimming events at the Montreal Games of 1976 taking out twelve of the thirteen races on the program. The sole exception was the victory of David Wilkie who hails from Scotland. In winning the 200-metre breaststroke, Wilkie became the first British male to secure an Olympic swimming title in sixty-eight years.

BOBBY MORROW

While it is now more than forty years since the Olympic Games were held in Melbourne, the name Bobby Morrow is still remembered by many Australians. It was Morrow who won the sprint double at the Melbourne Cricket Ground and this, combined with his membership of the winning 4 × 100-metre relay, earned him a haul of three gold medals from the 1956 Games.

Bob Morrow came to Melbourne after winning the US Olympic trials. He was then a student at the little known tertiary institution of Abilene Christian College.

In the 100-metre event Morrow went through all four rounds undefeated and won the final with a time of 10.5 seconds. Over the 200 metres he ran with a bandaged thigh but still managed to win in the Olympic record time of 20.6 seconds. In the relay he ran the anchor leg and booted home the US team to win from the Soviet team with Germany finishing third.

The year following his Olympic successes Morrow equalled the world record of 9.3 seconds for 100 yards on three separate occasions. One of the other people who had shared that time was Australia's Hec Hogan. Incidentally, Hogan had finished third to Morrow in the Olympic 100-metre final.

As recently as 1992, when the Games were held in Barcelona, there was an 11-year-old who represented his country. His name was Carlos Barrera and he competed for Spain in the sport of rowing. One suspects he was a cox!

ATLANTA 1996

Over the years, the Olympics have grown to be, without doubt, the largest sporting festival in the world. The following statistics from the Atlanta Olympics show just how big the event has now become.

In 1996, there were almost 201,000 people accredited to the Games.

The television pictures generated by the host broadcaster at the Atlanta Games totalled more than 3000 hours. For this coverage more than 460 kilometres of cabling was required to gain access to the various venues.

There were 1838 medals—gold, silver and bronze—used in victory ceremonies. Over 4 kilometres of ribbon was used for these medals.

More than 47,000 volunteers were accredited for the Games and they worked, on average, 117.6 hours.

Olympic pins were in abundance in Atlanta. Over 25,000 pins were sold every day during the Games, and at last count there were over 10,000 different designs from which to chose.

The five McDonald's which operated within the precincts of the Olympic village served over 150,000 Big Macs and Double Cheeseburgers. And while on the subject of food, 450,000 litres of milk were consumed and 400,000 slices of bread were used every day. And the ice required for athletes' needs exceeded 1.4 million kilograms.

Yes, the Olympic Games are B-I-G.

Andrew 'Boy' Charlton swam at three Olympic Games and won a gold medal for the 1500 metres in 1924. Yet in all his years of competition Charlton never swam in an Australian Championship.

JEAN-CLAUDE KILLY

The most famous competitor to emerge from the Winter Olympic Games of 1968 was Frenchman Jean-Claude Killy. At these Games, held in Grenoble, Killy emulated the triumphs of Austrian skier Toni Sailer by taking out all three Alpine events, the downhill, the slalom and the giant slalom.

While Sailer was by far the best skier at Cortina D'Ampezzo in 1956, dominating all his events, Killy's victories were not so clear cut. His wins in the slalom and the giant slalom were by less than a tenth of a second. Furthermore, his victory in the slalom came after the disqualification of another famous skier of the day, Austrian Karl Schranz.

Schranz had claimed that during his original run he had been baulked by the shadow of a policeman crossing the course. He was given another chance and his second run time would have secured him the gold medal. However, the French protested and after much deliberation, the jury decided not to allow Schranz's second time. This caused a major rift between the two leading Alpine countries, Austria and France, and had reverberations four years later in Sapporo.

Immediately following the Grenoble Games, Killy turned professional and made a lot of money by way of product endorsements. In 1992 he played a major role on the Organising Committee of the Albertville Winter Olympics and for this service he was made a member of the International Olympic Committee (IOC) in 1995.

> Pattie Dench from the south coast of NSW won a bronze medal for shooting at the Los Angeles Games in 1984 when she was fifty-two years of age and the mother of two sets of twins.

AUSTRALIA'S FORGOTTEN GOLD MEDALLIST

Donald Mackintosh is perhaps Australia's least known Olympic gold medallist. In fact, it has only been in recent years that his feats at the Paris Games of 1900 have been recognised by the Australian Olympic Committee and his gold medal status has been acknowledged.

Around the turn of the century Mackintosh was one of the world's finest shooters. He is considered the 'father' of shooting by the Australian Clay Pigeon Association and is honoured by membership in the Australian Sports Hall of Fame.

In 1900, this Melbourne gentleman found himself in Paris competing in the Prix Centenaire event which he won. While this contest did not have the word Olympic associated with it, there were many similar competitions which are recorded as being part of the second modern Games. It should be remembered that back then there were no national teams taking part in the Games and quite often, no national bodies in control of many sports. The Paris Games stretched over many months and they bore very little similarity to the Olympics that we know today.

The International Olympic Committee credits Mackintosh's gold medal to an archery event but it was actually for game shooting. Strangely enough, back then shooting was considered a discipline of archery.

Donald Mackintosh is also credited with a bronze medal from 1900. The IOC says he won this medal for live pigeon shooting.

For many years there was a shop in Elizabeth Street, Melbourne, which was called the Donald Mackintosh Gun Shop.

> At the first Games in Athens in 1896, there was a special swimming event for sailors.

BORZOV KNOWS THE ROPES

Many cynics of the Olympic movement often comment that the organisation which controls the Games—the International Olympic Committee—is made up of people who know very little about sport. This criticism cannot be levelled against the IOC member for Ukraine, Valeri Borzov.

Borzov was a wonderfully tuned sprinter who competed at two Olympic Games: Munich in 1972 and Montreal in 1976. In Munich he became the first European to win both the 100- and 200-metre titles which he did almost effortlessly. Some would say he did not face the best in the world at these Games as the two Americans, Eddie Hart and Reynaud Robinson, failed to turn up on time for the quarter-finals. But even if they had been there, this great Soviet athlete looked almost unbeatable.

Following the 1972 Olympics Borzov suffered both a psychological reaction and a muscle injury. However, by the time the European championships came around in 1974 he had recovered sufficiently to take out the 100-metre title.

Valeri Borzov went to the Montreal Games two years later and while not at his best, he still managed to pick up the bronze medal in the 100 metres. He was also on the USSR relay team which placed second in the 4 x100-metre event. This silver, along with the silver he won as a member of the same team in 1972, gave Borzov a grand total of two golds, two silvers and a bronze medal in Olympic competition.

In 1977 Borzov married the gymnast Ludmila Turischeva, herself a prolific Olympic medallist.

Valeri Borzov was made a member of the IOC in 1994.

EGYPTIAN DIVER

In the platform diving event at the Amsterdam Games of 1928 it appeared for a time that the Olympic champion would be Farid Simaika from Egypt. Simaika was announced as the winner and his national anthem was played to the assembled crowd. But then it was discovered a mistake had been made!

Only the ordinals or place-figures were to be counted in the determination of the gold medallist and the judges revised their decision. They awarded the victory to Pete Desjardins from the USA thus securing for the American his second gold of the Games. He had previously won the springboard diving event. This appears to have been a just decision as only one of the five judges ranked Simaika ahead of Desjardins in the tournament.

Following the Olympics the two placegetters teamed up and gave a series of exhibitions throughout Europe. Then, during World War II, Simaika took out American citizenship and joined the United States Army Air Corps. He was shot down over New Guinea.

> The record for the most appearances by a male at the Olympics is held by Paul Elvstrom of Denmark. He competed at eight Games in the sport of yachting. The record for most appearances by a female is held by Kerstin Palm who fenced at seven consecutive Games (1964–1988) for her native Sweden.

LESLIE BOARDMAN— OLYMPIC CHAMPION

Possibly the least known of Australia's long line of Olympic swimming gold medallists is Leslie Boardman. Boardman was a member of our victorious 4 x 200-metre freestyle relay at the Stockholm Games of 1912.

When the original team was announced to go to Sweden, Boardman's name was not among those chosen. Swimming had only selected three male competitors, Cecil Healy, Harold Hardwick and Bill Longworth. It was anticipated a fourth swimmer would be added later on.

Initially, the name of E.G. Finlay from Western Australia was put forward but it appears he could not raise the money required to go away. Then the name of Leslie Boardman was mentioned and he joined his three NSW compatriots.

Boardman's selection was a strange one. He had not placed in any of the Australian championship races of 1912 and his best showing in the NSW state titles was a fourth. The apparent reason for his addition was that he was a team-mate of Hardwick's and Healy's at the Sydney Swimming Club.

Leslie Boardman swam in two events in Stockholm. He contested the 100-metre freestyle where he made it through to the second round. But it was as a member of the 4 x 200-metre relay that he gained his moment of glory.

Swimming the third leg for Australasia, he lengthened the lead set up by Healy and Malcolm Champion (NZ) enabling Harold Hardwick to hold off a challenge from the great Duke Kahanamoku. Thus, this relative unknown became an Olympic gold medallist!

DECATHLETES AS ACTORS

The decathlon has always been one of the most popular events on the Olympic program. This two-day contest is made up of ten different competitions, all of which take place in the Olympic Stadium.

On the first day, athletes take part in the 100 metres, the long jump, the shot-put, the high jump and the 400 metres. The next day they compete in the disciplines of the 110-metre hurdles, the discus, the pole vault, the javelin and finish with a gruelling 1500-metre run.

Because of the popularity of the decathlon, many of the winners and 'stars' who have performed well over the years have found their way into movies.

Jim Thorpe, the American Indian who won both the decathlon and pentathlon at Stockholm in 1912, played an extra in several early Hollywood Westerns.

Glenn Morris from the USA, the winner of the event at the Berlin Games of 1936, appeared in two B-grade movies, *Tarzan's Revenge* and *Hold That Co-Ed*.

Bob Mathias, perhaps the greatest of all decathletes, and winner of both the 1948 and 1952 Olympic competitions, starred opposite Jayne Mansfield in *It Happened in Athens*.

At the 1948 US Olympic trials, there was another young aspiring actor who fancied himself as a decathlete. While the individual could only finish sixth at these trials he did go on to gain some fame as an actor. His name was Dennis Weaver and he is remembered for his roles in the television series *Gunsmoke* and *McCloud*.

> While no females competed at the first Olympics in Athens in 1896, two Greek women ran unofficially in the marathon.

OLDEST BOXING GOLD

The oldest man to win an Olympic gold medal in boxing was 37-year-old Richard Gunn. At the 1908 London Games, Gunn won the featherweight title.

Gunn had been the British amateur champion between 1894 and 1896. He was so superior in his weight class that whenever he entered a tournament, others withdrew. Hence, officials asked him to retire from all competition. Gunn was known for his sportsmanship and complied with the request.

When the London Olympics rolled around, he decided to come out of retirement. He defeated one Frenchman and two Englishmen to win the gold medal.

Richard Gunn ended up retiring for good after the Olympics boasting a very proud record of having lost only one fight in fifteen years.

To give you some idea of just how the Games have grown over the past forty years it is interesting to compare figures from the 1956 Melbourne Olympics and the anticipated numbers for Sydney in 2000. At Melbourne there were 3184 athletes representing sixty-seven countries. In Sydney it is estimated there will be 10,300 athletes from some 200 countries.

GOLDS AT SUMMER AND WINTER OLYMPICS

The light heavyweight division in boxing was first held in Olympic competition at the Antwerp Games of 1920. The winner on that occasion was Eddie Eagan from the United States.

Eagan grew up in Denver, Colorado, and in spite of coming from a poor family, he managed to attend some of the most prestigious universities in the country. He went to Yale for his undergraduate work followed by Harvard Law School. Upon getting his law degree he travelled to Oxford and eventually went into practice and became a very successful lawyer.

Eagan admired the fictional hero of dime store novels, Frank Merriwell. He patterned his social behaviour on this character and never smoked or drank alcohol.

Eddie Eagan returned to the Olympic arena twelve years after his boxing title. At the 1932 winter Games, held at Lake Placid, he competed in the four-man bobsled event for the USA. This team went on to victory thus making Eagan a very rare sportsman—someone who has won gold medals at both the Summer and Winter Olympic Games.

> Jimmy Carruthers, who was to go on and become world champion when he turned professional, took part in the bantamweight division of the boxing competition at the London Games of 1948. He had to withdraw after he suffered a cut eye.

DEAN LUKIN

Dean Lukin, competing in the super heavyweight division at the 1984 Games in Los Angeles, won Australia's first and only Olympic gold medal in weightlifting.

Lukin came from the small fishing community of Port Lincoln in South Australia. Going into the LA competition he was considered a very strong chance for victory because of the Soviet boycott of the American Games. However, his confidence was stripped away when he contracted a stomach virus a few weeks before the start of the Games. Lukin lost over five kilograms.

The 'gentle giant' decided not to march in the Opening Ceremony so as to conserve his energy. Instead, he spent a lot of time in the dining halls of the village eating two or three steaks at a sitting.

By the time his event had come around on 8 August, Lukin had regained the lost weight and went into the competition as the heaviest of the lifters at 138.5 kg.

The South Australian's main opposition was Mario Martinez from the USA. Martinez was first in the 'snatch' section but when it came to the 'clean and jerk' Lukin came into his own. His first lift of 227 kg assured him of at least a silver. He then called for 240 kg. Rather than struggling, he made it look simple. He made the 'clean' with ease, 'jerked' it above his head and held it. When he eventually dropped the weight to the floor, he was Olympic champion.

The Australian team manager, Bill Hoffman, recognised Lukin's magnificent effort by rewarding him with the honour of carrying the flag in the Closing Ceremony. Hoffman told Dean that if he carried it one-handed around the stadium, he could keep the flag. This he did.

The people of Port Lincoln went wild over the knowledge that one of their own was an Olympic gold medallist and for a short time the town was renamed Port Lukin. Today Dean Lukin has lost much of the bulk he carried when he achieved his Olympic victory. In fact, he is such a svelte figure you would hardly recognise him as the same man.

> The winners of the modern pentathlon events in 1920 and 1928, Gustaf Dyrssen and Sven Thofelt respectively, both became members of the Swedish épée team which picked up a silver medal at the Berlin Games of 1936. Thofelt went on to compete in London some twelve years later and added to his gold and silver medals with a bronze, once again in the team épée event. Both men were later to become members of the International Olympic Committee.

BOB HAYES— SPRINTING GIANT

American Bob Hayes was the first man to run 100 yards in 9.1 seconds. Going into the 1964 Olympic Games, Hayes had forty-eight straight victories over this distance and the metric equivalent, 100 metres.

The three favourites to take out the medals in Tokyo were the American, Cuba's Enrique Figuerola and Canada's Harry Jerome. When the gun went off these three leapt out of the blocks and were clear of the rest of the field at the 10-metre mark. But then Hayes pulled out all stops and shot to the lead. He was ahead by a metre at the halfway point and ended up winning by a massive two metres; the proverbial 'country mile' in the short distance sprint.

Both Figuerola and Jerome had nothing but praise for Hayes' victory and heralded him as the greatest sprinter of all time.

Immediately after the Olympics Bob Hayes turned professional and began a career in American football. He played nine years for the Dallas Cowboys and was so fast the opposition had to invent a new strategy, the zone defence, in order to stop him.

After retiring from football Hayes began to 'hit the bottle' and in 1978 was arrested for selling cocaine. The following year he was sent to prison and spent ten months in a Texas gaol. Upon his release he once again drifted back to alcohol and drugs but finally underwent successful rehabilitation.

In 1994 this Olympic great earned a degree in elementary education from Florida A & M University. He was fifty-one years of age.

LIS HARTEL

Lis Hartel was one of Denmark's leading equestrian riders and due to have a child when she contracted polio and became partially paralysed. But she was determined this would not stop her. Lis learned to lift her arm and regained the use of her thigh muscles. Then she gave birth to a healthy daughter. But this remarkable lady was not finished. She insisted on riding again and while she remained paralysed below the knees, she learned to do without these muscles. At the 1952 Helsinki Olympics, Lis Hartel won the silver medal, even though she had to be helped on and off her horse. When gold medallist Henri Saint Cyr helped Lis onto the victory platform it was one of the most emotional moments in Olympic history.

While Bobby Pearce had won his first gold medal at the Amsterdam Games of 1928, he was ruled ineligible to compete in the diamond sculls event at Henley-on-Thames in 1929. This event was open only to people considered to be 'gentlemen' and as Pearce was a carpenter who worked with his hands, he did not fit the definition.

AUSTRALIA AT THE OLYMPIC GAMES

Australia has the very proud record of being one of only two countries to have competed at every modern Summer Olympic Games since their inception in 1896. The other country is Greece.

During the 100 years of Olympic competition Australia has managed to win medals of some kind or other at every Games except St Louis in 1904. The number of medals have ranged from a single bronze at Berlin in 1936 to our record haul in Atlanta of forty-one. In total, this nation has won 292 medals at the Olympics comprising eighty-nine gold, eighty-five silver and 118 bronze.

Swimming has been the most successful sport in terms of delivering the most number of medals. Our swimmers, over the years, have brought home 123 medals, forty of which have been gold. In fact, it has been at only two Games that our swimmers were not successful. These were the first Games in Athens and the 1936 Berlin Olympics.

Athletics, or track and field as it is known throughout most of the world, is our next most successful sport. With the likes of Betty Cuthbert, Marjorie Jackson and Shirley Strickland our athletes have contributed some fifty-nine medals, eighteen of which have been gold.

> The site of the ancient Games, Olympia, was rediscovered by Englishman Richard Chandler in 1760.

With Sydney looming, it would be a safe bet to say that all these numbers will be added to following the 2000 Games.

POLITICS AND SPORT

Who said politics doesn't enter into sport?

At the 1972 Munich Olympic Games a North Korean, Li Ho-jun, won the gold medal in the small-bore rifle in the prone position. He defeated Victor Auer of the United States and set a new world record with a near perfect score of 599 points.

Following Li's victory, a press conference was held. At this conference reporters wanted to know to what Li attributed his win. The thoroughly indoctrinated communist said he imagined he was shooting at his enemies. He went on tell the assembled world media that his leader and Prime Minister, Kim-Il Sung, had told the Korean team 'to shoot as if we were fighting our enemies'.

Obviously this statement did not go over too well and it was considered to be unsportsmanlike. The North Korean team management picked up on this and scheduled a second press conference. At this gathering Li said he had been misquoted and recanted his earlier view.

The second placegetter Auer was an interesting figure in his own right. He was a Hollywood scriptwriter and had written for such TV classics as *Gunsmoke* and *Bonanza*.

Women were allowed to compete in the 'arduous' sport of track and field for the first time in 1928. This was some sixteen years after their sisters first took to the swimming pool in Olympic competition.

MODERN PENTATHLON

Lars Hall of Sweden holds a special place in the history of the sport of modern pentathlon.

In 1952, at the Games held in Helsinki, Finland, Hall became the first nonmilitary winner of the Olympic event. At these Games he had two very fortunate situations which helped him attain his victory. First, the horse he initially drew for the equestrian section of the competition was discovered to be lame. When he was given his substitute horse, that animal turned out to be the best horse in all of Finland. Hall's only duty was to stay 'on board' and keep from falling off, and this is what he did.

Two days later the Swede turned up twenty minutes late for the pistol shooting contest. This should have meant disqualification but as luck would have it, the event had not started as a jury was investigating a Soviet protest.

Four years later, in Melbourne, Lars Hall was again the winner. With this gold medal Hall became immortalised in his sport as he is the only person ever to win two Olympic modern pentathlon events.

During the 1960 Olympic team time trial, Danish cyclist Knut Jensen collapsed and died. It was later found that he had taken a drug which acted as a blood circulation stimulant. Jensen was the first person to die in Olympic competition since the marathon race of 1912.

FREDDIE LANE

In recent years, Australia has produced many Olympic gold medallists in the sport of swimming. The names of Rose, Fraser and Perkins are now household words but our very first Olympic swimming champion was the diminutive Freddie Lane, way back in 1900 at the first Paris Games.

Lane not only won the 200-metre freestyle but went on to take out the 200-metre obstacle race. This event was held in the River Seine and the swimmers had to clamber across rowing boats and under punts which were moored in the stream.

Lane had been raised by a ship's chandler in his home town of Sydney and understood a lot about boats. He knew it was easier to climb over the boats at the stern rather than scramble over the sides as most of his rivals did. This gave him a distinct advantage and allowed him to win one of the most unique gold medals in Olympic history.

Freddie Lane was only a small man weighing a mere 59.9 kg. However, he stands tall in the Olympic movement.

I had the great pleasure of meeting this wonderful man in 1960. He died in 1979.

In the sport of weightlifting, where size is important, American Joseph de Pietro must rate a mention. In London in 1948, this American bantamweight became the smallest ever Olympic champion. He was only 1.42 metres (4 feet 8 inches) tall yet set a world record taking out the gold.

OLYMPIC FLAG

The Olympic flag was first flown in Alexandria, Greece, in 1914 at the time of the Pan-Egyptian Games. The design of the flag incorporates five interlaced rings, of differing colours, on a white background. The colours, blue, yellow, black, green and red, represent colours from the flags of all nations in the Olympic movement at that time.

The founder of the modern Olympics, Baron Pierre de Coubertin, submitted the design for the flag in 1913. It was approved by the International Olympic Committee and the first flag was made by the Bon Marche stores in Paris.

Following the Pan-Egyptian Games, the flag was used in Paris at the time of the 20th anniversary of the revival of the Olympic movement.

It was at the Games of the seventh Olympiad at Antwerp, Belgium, in 1920 that the flag was first hoisted over an Olympic venue. On that occasion the flag bore the famous motto 'Citius, Altius, Fortius' which means 'Faster, Higher, Stronger'.

One of the more interesting performances at an Olympic Games was in the 800 metres at the Montreal Olympics. Running in the second heat of the first round was one Wilnor Joseph of Haiti. His time of 2 minutes 15.26 seconds was so slow that it would not have qualified him for the final in 1900, let alone in 1976.

THE MANLY CONNECTION

Australia won three gold medals at the 1924 'Chariots of Fire' Olympic Games in Paris and all the victors came from the same Sydney suburb of Manly.

The great Andrew 'Boy' Charlton won his only gold medal in Olympic competition in the 1500-metre freestyle.

Richmond Eve took out Australia's first and only diving gold medal when he won the plain high diving event.

And Nick Winter was a surprise winner in the hop, step and jump.

All three lived within a mile radius of each other at Manly and when they returned from the Games they were given a street parade in the seaside suburb. They even had avenues named after them!

Another Manly Olympian was Ernest Henry. Ernie was a member of the 4 × 200-metre relay team which won a silver medal.

The sport of roque, a form of croquet, had its moment of glory when it was part of the program at the St Louis Games of 1904. It has never been played, and dare I say, never been heard of, since.

BENJAMIN SPOCK

Nearly every modern-day parent has had some exposure to a book called *The Common Sense Book of Baby Child Care*. This book is considered the bible in matters of child raising and was written by a Dr Benjamin Spock.

Back in 1924, Ben Spock was a gawky young medical student attending Yale University. He was also a rower and as a member of America's rowing eight at the Paris Olympics, he won a gold medal.

After graduating from medical school Spock became a paediatrician and in 1945 he published his now famous book. Since then it has sold over twenty-five million copies and gained for its author international fame as the world's foremost expert on babies.

Over the years the dominant country in men's hockey has been India. They won their first gold medal at the 1928 Games in Amsterdam and held the Olympic crown until Pakistan beat them in 1960. The man who led India to its first three victories was captain Dhyan Chand. He later went on to coach his nation's team.

AUSTRALIA AT THE WINTER GAMES

While Australia can lay claim to being one of only two countries to have had teams at every Summer Games, this same honour cannot be bestowed on our Winter Olympic representation. The first Winter Games were held at Chamonix, France, in 1924 but it was another twelve years before we fielded a cold-weather team.

The first Australian team member to take part in a Winter Olympics was Kenneth Kennedy who competed in the speed skating events in 1936. The Games were held that year in Garmisch-Partenkirchen, Germany, and they took on many of the characteristics of that year's Summer Olympics in Berlin and are sometimes referred to as the Nazi Winter Olympics.

There was another Australian at those Games, Freddie McEvoy (he was a friend of the flamboyant actor, Errol Flynn), who competed for Great Britain. McEvoy took part in both the four-man and two-man bobsled events.

Australia failed to send a team to the first Winter Games following World War II but since 1952 we have had continuous and strong teams competing at Winter Olympics.

Over the years there have been many well-known names who have worn the green and gold in the snow. There was Colin Coates who took part in six consecutive Olympics; Jim Lynch, the speed skater who once held the world record; figure skaters Danielle and Stephen Carr who only finished their careers at the Nagano Games; and, of course, the 'father' of the Australian Winter Olympic movement, leading AOC official Geoff Henke.

In recent times the likes of Steven Lee and Kirstie Marshall have been touted as potential medal winners but it took until 1994, at the Games in Lillehammer, for Australia to pick up its first Winter

Olympic medal. At those Games, the short track ice racing team of Steven Bradbury, Kieran Hansen, Andrew Mutha and Richard Nizielski, along with John Kah as a reserve, broke through and won a bronze medal in the 5000-metre event.

At the time, one prominent Australian Olympic official stated that this third place medal was the most important achievement in our Olympic development since the gold medal of Edwin Flack in 1896.

In 1998 Australia won its second Winter medal when the alpine skier Zali Steggal, from the Sydney beachside suburb of Manly, took out the third placing in the slalom.

One of the stars of the second modern Games in Paris (1900) was Alvin Kraenziein from the United States. He won four gold medals—the long jump, 60-metre sprint, the 110-metre hurdles and the 200-metre hurdles. If Alvin was competing today he would be a superstar and undoubtedly a very wealthy man.

GREG LOUGANIS

Greg Louganis is an American of Samoan and European ancestry. He had a difficult childhood. He began smoking when he was eight and by the time he was a teenager he was an alcoholic. But Louganis survived the hard times and found the sport of diving.

He went to the Montreal Olympics at the age of sixteen and won a silver medal in platform diving. As the 1980 Moscow Games loomed he was the red-hot favourite to take out gold in the two diving events. However, as history recalls, the United States boycotted the 1980 Olympics over the question of Afghanistan.

Four years later, at the Los Angeles Games, Louganis was invincible in both the springboard and platform diving. He became the first platform diver to score over 700 points and the first male since 1928 to win both diving events.

In the Seoul Games of 1988, while diving in the preliminary rounds of the springboard, Louganis hit his head on the board. He had four stitches inserted in the gash and went back and qualified for the final. The next day Louganis earned his third Olympic gold medal!

Greg Louganis went on to take out the platform event and thus became the first male in Olympic history to win both diving events in back-to-back Games.

While swimming is a very popular sport here in Australia, no swimmer in Olympic history has been called upon to take the Olympic oath. In Melbourne in 1956, Australian athlete John Landy recited the oath.

JIM THORPE

Jim Thorpe was an American Indian who attended the Carlisle Indian school in Pennsylvania in the first decade of the twentieth century. It was while at Carlisle that he developed his talent for athletics.

Thorpe was selected to go to the 1912 Olympic Games in Stockholm, and won both the pentathlon and decathlon events. He also finished fourth in the high jump and seventh in the long jump.

Then it was discovered that some years before, Thorpe had earned $25 a week for playing minor league baseball. His Olympic medals were taken away and his name stricken from all record books.

In 1950, an American poll voted Thorpe the Greatest Athlete of the Century and a film was made about him starring Burt Lancaster.

In 1971, 400,000 people signed a petition to reinstate Thorpe as an Olympic champion and in 1982 the International Olympic Committee recognised his Olympic feats. His Olympic medals were presented to Thorpe's children by the president of the IOC the following year.

Thorpe himself had died a poor man in 1953.

> The prize for the winners at the ancient Games was a simple olive branch. The olive tree was considered sacred by the Greeks and the power and vitality of the branch was thought to have been passed on to the athlete.

DUKE KAHANAMOKU

The Hawaiian Duke Paoa Kahanamoku is generally credited with introducing the sport of surfboard riding to Australia. But few surfers would know that the great Duke was also a dual Olympic champion.

The Duke won back-to-back gold medals in the 100-metre freestyle at the Stockholm Games of 1912 and the Antwerp Games of 1920.

In 1912, due to a misunderstanding, Kahanamoku missed his semi-final race. However, Australian Cecil Healy insisted on an extra race being conducted and the Duke made it into the final.

Ironically, this gesture by Healy cost him the gold medal. In the final he finished second. If the Hawaiian had not swum, it would have been the Australian who would have won.

A statue of the great Duke was recently erected overlooking Freshwater Beach on Sydney's northern peninsula to commemorate the venue where he taught Australians how to surf.

Jim Carlton, father of radio broadcaster Mike Carlton, was Australia's number one sprinter in the late 1920s and early 1930s. Twice he beat one of the world's best in George Simpson. In Amsterdam he went through to the second round of both the 100 metres and 200 metres. Just prior to the 1932 Los Angeles Games, when he was at his best, Carlton entered the priesthood. Carlton eventually left the priesthood and had a family.

FLO-JO

Without doubt, the star of the 1988 Olympic Games in Seoul, Korea, would have to have been Florence Griffith Joyner, better known to the world as Flo-Jo.

This flamboyant American, who won both the sprint events on the track and picked up a third gold as a member of the winning 400-metre relay team, became a household name, not only in her native country but in every nation around the world that saw the television coverage of those Games.

However, it was not so much her athletic performances that attracted attention. It was the fact that she wore figure-hugging racing suits and adorned herself with brightly coloured fingernails and outrageously long eyelashes that gained her the notice of the world press.

Because of her rapid improvement between 1986 and 1988, and also the disqualification of Ben Johnson for the use of steroids, there was much talk about Flo-Jo being aided in her performaces at Seoul by drugs. Her bulging muscles also prompted talk about possible drug abuse. However, this striking black queen of the track passed every drug test she ever took.

Flo-Jo's sister-in-law, Jackie Joyner-Kersee, won two gold medals at the Seoul Olympics, being victorious in the heptathlon and the long jump.

> Australian walker Noel Freeman won a silver medal for the 20-kilometre race at Rome in 1960. However, that silver could very well have been gold had he been given proper directions as well as indications of just how far he was from the leader.

FOUL PLAY

The 10,000-metre final at the 1992 Barcelona Olympics was considered a severe body blow to the Olympic spirit. The final developed into a one-on-one battle between Richard Chelimo of Kenya and Morocco's Khalid Skah. Skah took the lead after nineteen laps before mysteriously pulling wide and allowing Chelimo to pass on the inside. Up ahead, waiting to be lapped, was Skah's countryman and henchman Hammou Boutayeb. In the next lap and a half, Boutayeb twice swung out when the Kenyan tried to pass, forcing him to break stride, change direction and pass inside. In addition, the Kenyan said he was knocked off balance, bumped three times and elbowed. Skah won but was disqualified. The Moroccans appealed and he was reinstated, but he faced constant heckling when receiving his gold medal at the victory ceremony.

While the sport of equestrian has produced some marvellous characters over the years, none was more charismatic than the Dutch rider of the 1920s and 1930s with the wonderful name of Charles F. Pahud de Mortanges. Riding his beautiful mount Marcroix, de Mortanges won the individual three-day event gold medal at the 1928 and 1932 Olympics and received team golds in 1924 and 1928.

VASSILY ALEXEYEV

Between 1970 and 1977, the Soviet weightlifter Vassily Alexeyev set an amazing eighty world records. He also won two Olympic gold medals and established himself as one of the all-time greats of his sport.

This mammoth super heavyweight came to international attention in early 1970 when he broke the world record for the press, the jerk and the three-lift total. Shortly after, he became the first person in history to lift a combined total of 600 kg.

At the Munich Olympic Games of 1972 Alexeyev lifted 640 kg—30 kg more than the second placegetter. Rumour has it that he performed other enormous feats in the Olympic village. He was spotted one morning having a 'light' breakfast of twenty-six fried eggs and a steak.

Four years later at Montreal, Alexeyev was again in a class of his own and this time finished 35 kg ahead of the field in the two-lift total.

It is interesting to note that Vassily Alexeyev wife's name was Olympiada.

Every modern Olympiad is consecutively numbered from 1896, the year of the first Games in Athens. Despite the wartime cancellations of the sixth, twelfth and thirteenth Olympiads, the numbers are still recorded in history.

JUMPS FOR HORSES

There were once high jump and long jump events in the Olympic Games... for horses! Both events were held at the 1900 Paris Games.

The equine high jump was won by Frenchman Dominique Mawimien Garderes on his horse Canela with a jump of 1.85 metres.

The long jump winner at these Games was the Belgian Constant van Langhendonck on his horse Extra Dry, clearing 6.10 metres.

This was the only time these Olympic events were held.

Cyril Mackworth-Praed placed second in the Running Deer Shooting competition in Paris in 1924. Twenty-eight years later, when he was sixty, Mackworth-Praed competed at Helsinki and finished eleventh in the trap event. However, it was not as a shooter that the Englishman made his mark. He was a noted ornithologist and spent the best part of forty years compiling the distinguished six-volume work, *African Handbook of Birds*.

HERB ELLIOTT

In the sport of track and field there is no greater name than Australia's Herb Elliott. As a senior, he was never defeated over the mile or 1500 metres and he won forty-four consecutive races.

But it was for his performance at the 1960 Rome Olympics that the world will remember him. Before 90,000 spectators in the magnificent Stadio Olympico, Elliott spreadeagled the field and won the 1500 metres in 3 minutes 35.6 seconds.

The West Australian was first exposed to the Olympics when he was taken to Melbourne by his father for the 1956 Games. Sitting in the stands at the Melbourne Cricket Ground, Elliott saw Vladimir Kuts win the 5000- and 10,000-metre events. These victories inspired the young athlete and he decided to take up an offer to train under the eccentric coach Percy Cerutty in the Portsea sandhills.

By 1958, Elliott had blossomed into one of the leading middle distance runners in the world. He went to the British Empire Games in Cardiff, and won both the 880-yard and mile races.

Two years later in Rome, Herb Elliott ran what is still considered to be the greatest 1500-metre race ever run. He beat the second placegetter, Frenchman Michael Jazy, by the whopping time of 2.8 seconds and his win was the most decisive in Olympic history.

Standing on the dais after he received his gold medal, Elliott recalled many years later, 'The pride that filled my heart, on that day, was for my country, not myself.'

Following the World Championships in Rome in 1987, athletes, officials, statisticians and journalists voted Herb Elliott the greatest 1500-metre runner of the past seventy-five years.

BORIS ONISCHENKO

One man who became famous at the 1976 Montreal Olympics was the Soviet Army's Major Boris Onischenko. But Boris was elevated to great heights for the wrong reasons. In fact, he became infamous at these Games because he cheated.

Onischenko was a member of the USSR's modern pentathlon team. While fencing against Great Britain, his opponent noticed something odd about the defending silver medallist. The automatic light registered a hit for him even though he did not appear to have touched his rival.

It happened again when he faced his next combatant and it soon became obvious something was amiss! His épée was taken from him and examined by officials.

Evidently Onischenko, desperate for victory, had wired his sword with a concealed push-button circuit-breaker which enabled him to register a hit whenever he wanted.

He was immediately disqualified and was spirited out of the Olympic village, never to be seen outside the Soviet Union again.

> The first Games following World War I were those held at Antwerp in 1920. Included on the equestrian program that year were events for individual and teams figure riding. These events were open only to Army officers and included such intricate manoeuvres as jumping on and off a horse, standing on your mount and jumping over horses.

TWINS WIN GOLD ON SAME DAY

One of the most unusual family performances at any Olympics was that of Australia's Anderson brothers, John and Tom, who won gold medals as crewmen in yachting events at the 1972 Munich Games.

These identical twins were racing in different events on the same day. John sailed with skipper David Forbes to win the Star class. Brother Tom was with skipper John Cuneo and John Shaw in the winning Dragon class.

The Andersons grew up in Brisbane near the St Lucia ferry crossing on the Brisbane River and the boys learned to swim there. They also learned to row and used to cross the river in their father's rowboat to gather and sell mushrooms.

As their father was a bootmaker, the family could not afford to buy a sailing boat so the twins decided to build their own. In all, they built seven sailing boats, selling them at the end of each season and upgrading the next year.

John got to know David Forbes during the lead-up to the 1970 America's Cup campaign. He gained valuable experience crewing on both *Gretel II* and *Vim*. In 1972 Forbes and Anderson purchased the hull of a Star and fitted it out to their personal requirements. They named the boat *Scallywag*.

Tom spent his honeymoon in 1970 at the Flying Dutchman class World Championships. In 1972 he joined Cuneo and prepared for their assault on the Olympic gold in the Dragon class.

Harry Gordon, who in 1994 published the official history of Australia at the Olympics, has found in his research that a pair of Norwegian twins, Jorg and Bernd Landvoigt, won gold at the following Games in 1976—in the pair-oared shell with cox. The difference about the Andersons' golds was that they were won on the same day in different races.

Incidentally, Australia had another pair of identical twins at the Montreal Olympics. Salvatore and Remo Sansonetti were members of the cycling team which finished ninth in the 100 km time trial.

> The athletic events at the first Paris Games (1900) were held at Bois de Boulogne. This was a beautiful property owned by the Racing Club of France and it presented some unique problems for many of the athletes. The discus throwers had to attempt to throw their implements straight down a lane of trees; the hurdlers found themselves having to leap over old telephone poles; and the javelin competitors often found their 'spears' lodged in the branches of surrounding trees.

FANNY DURACK

Fanny Durack was Australia's first female Olympic champion. She took out the gold medal in the 100-metre freestyle event at the Stockholm Games of 1912. However, she won her crown at a time when women swimmers in this country competed under the most difficult of circumstances.

The forerunner of our great champions Lorraine Crapp, Dawn Fraser, Shane Gould and Tracey Wickham, Fanny Durack swam at a time when women were not allowed to race at carnivals if male spectators were present. In fact, large signs were displayed outside baths forbidding men to enter when the women were swimming.

Fanny was also hampered by restrictions on the swimming costumes women could wear at the time. And of course, women swimmers were prohibited from travelling without female chaperones.

At Stockholm, Fanny (real name, Sarah), won her heat, semi-final and final of the 100-metre freestyle and broke the world record twice on her way to the gold medal. Her good friend Mina Wylie, after whom the famous Wylie Baths at Coogee in Sydney are named, took the silver.

The fame of the two Australian girls spread around the world. Fanny and Mina toured America three times over the next few years and helped to break down many of the taboos which prevented women from taking part in elite competitions.

As the Antwerp Games of 1920 approached, Fanny trained hard. It was her intention to defend her Olympic title but a week before the Australians were to go overseas, she had to have her appendix removed. Complications followed and she was forced to retire.

BETTY CUTHBERT

Betty Cuthbert was a youthful 18-year-old when she went to Melbourne in 1956 to compete in the Olympic Games. She was chosen with her team-mate Marlene Mathews to run in both sprint events in the first Games to be held in the Southern Hemisphere.

The daughter of an Ermington, Sydney, nurseryman, Betty took the world by storm at those Games and at their completion, the Melbourne *Argus* proclaimed her as Australia's 'Golden Girl'. This shy, inexperienced blonde 'flash' had won three Olympic gold medals.

Before the Games, Cuthbert was not considered a threat to the Germans Christina Stubnik and Gisela Kohler. But in the final of the 100 metres she streaked away from Stubnik and Mathews and took out the gold.

Four days later, Betty earned another Olympic gold when she won the 200-metre final, again beating Stubnick and Mathews. It's the only time in Games history the medallists in both sprint events have finished in exactly the same order.

Later she won a third gold by being a member of the victorious 4 x 100-metre relay.

Eight years later Betty won a fourth gold medal in the 400 metres at the Tokyo Olympics. This race brought her running career to an end and closed the chapter on the sporting history of one of Australia's greatest champions.

Betty Cuthbert is now suffering from the debilitating disease of multiple sclerosis and lives quietly in Mandurah, Western Australia.

> The first perfect score of 10 in Olympic gymnastic competition was awarded to Romania's Nadia Comaneci at Montreal in 1976.

JACK KELLY

Most Australians will have heard of the Hollywood actress Grace Kelly, the beautiful American film star who endeared herself to the film-going public in the 1950s. She later went on to meet, and marry, Prince Rainier of Monaco and for the remainder of her life lived in the small Mediterranean principality. However, what most Australians probably don't know is that Princess Grace of Monaco had a very famous father who was an Olympic rowing champion.

Jack Kelly was a Philadelphia bricklayer who won 126 straight rowing races. He was intent on taking out the most prestigious of all rowing events, the diamond sculls at Henley, England.

In 1920, Kelly prepared himself for this big event but he was barred from competing because his rowing club had been accused of participating in professional races.

A few weeks later, at the Antwerp Olympics, Kelly took on the diamond sculls winner, Jack Beresford, in the final of the single sculls event and beat him. This competition was so draining on both men, however, that they could not even shake hands at the end of the race. They were too exhausted! Nevertheless, Kelly managed to recover sufficiently to win a second gold medal in the double sculls event a mere thirty minutes later.

Four years later, Jack Kelly returned to the Olympic arena and at the 1924 Games in Paris he successfully defended his double sculls title.

Jack Kelly's son John competed in four Olympic Games in rowing events and brought great joy to his father when in 1947 he won the diamond sculls—something his father had been denied.

> The Japanese women's volleyball team at the Montreal Games of 1976 was so strong that only once did an opponent get to double figures in a single game.

EMIL ZATOPEK

Czechoslovakia's Emil Zatopek won a gold medal at his first appearance at an Olympic Games. It was at the London Games of 1948 and he won the prestigious 10,000-metre event. He also finished second in the 5000 metres. However, it was four years later that Zatopek stamped himself as one of the all-time greats of track and field.

At the 1952 Helsinki Games he won both the 5000- and 10,000-metre races and then decided to tackle the marathon, an event he had never run before.

Zatopek knew that Britain's Jim Peters was the prerace favourite. He found Peters' singlet number in a newspaper and decided to run alongside him throughout the race.

As the event progressed, it became apparent the Czech runner was far superior to anyone else in the race. He went on to win the marathon so easily that he was already signing autographs when the next runner entered the stadium.

Zatopek had a unique running style and his face was always contorted, as if he was in extreme pain. When asked if this was the case, he answered, 'No, I just wasn't talented enough to run and smile at the same time!'

Emil Zatopek won four Olympic gold medals but has only three in his possession. In 1966, he gave one to Australia's Ron Clarke who had broken so many world records but never won a gold medal. Zatopek felt Clarke deserved one of his.

In 1968, Zatopek signed the 2000 Words Manifesto supporting the establishment of freedom in Czechoslovakia. For that, he was expelled from the Army, in which he was a lieutenant-colonel. The only work he could find was labouring.

Emil Zatopek and his wife Dana, an Olympic javelin gold medallist, lived as persona non grata in their homeland until the 1990 collapse of the communist government.

The hammer throw was introduced into the Olympics in 1900. The man who won the event the first three times it was held (1900, 1904 and 1908) was New York policeman John Flanagan. The Irish-born Flanagan returned to his country of birth in 1911 and died there in 1938.

DUNC GRAY

Australia has produced many great cyclists but perhaps none greater than Olympic gold medallist Edgar Laurence 'Dunc' Gray.

Dunc won his gold in the 1000-metre time trial at the first Los Angeles Games in 1932, however he had an international career which spanned the period from 1928 until 1938.

As a 22-year-old he competed at the Amsterdam Olympics of 1928. He came away with the bronze medal in the time trial but still believes he had a better time than the second placegetter and should have received the silver.

At Los Angeles four years later, Gray was the sole Australian cycling competitor. He entered both the time trial and the 1000-metre scratch race. He made it through to the race-off for third place in the scratch race but realised he could not win a gold or silver, so decided to withdraw, conserving his energy for the time trial.

When the time trial event came around on 3 August, Dunc was one of nine to take to the track in pursuit of the gold medal. He knew he had to ride a time he had never ridden before if he was to be successful.

By the time he finished the flying kilometre Gray had recorded a time of 1 minute 13.0 seconds, breaking the world record and slashing almost three seconds off the Olympic record. Australia had won its first gold medal in cycling!

Four years later Dunc was Australia's flag-bearer at the Berlin Games but the whole experience of competing in Nazi Germany was very upsetting. Years later, while launching a history of Australians at the Olympics, the octogenarian recalled what went through his mind upon seeing Hitler. If he had gone through with action he contemplated with the flag-bearer's pole, then possibly the course of history may have been changed.

Dunc Gray finished his international competitive career in front of a home town crowd. He won the gold medal for the 1000-metre sprint at the British Empire Games of Sydney in 1938.

> At the 1976 Olympics in Montreal athletes from three different Caribbean countries took out the 100-metre, 200-metre and 800-metre events on the track. In the 100 it was Hasley Crawford from Trinidad; the 200 was won by Donald Quarrie of Jamaica; and the 800 went to Alberto Juantorena from Cuba.

SNOWY BAKER

Snowy Baker is unquestionably the greatest all-round athlete Australia has ever produced. He competed at state or national level in twenty-nine different sports. He played halfback in two rugby Tests against England and was also national amateur middleweight boxing champion. In the 1908 London Olympics, Baker won a boxing silver medal and also took part in the springboard diving and 4 x 200-metre freestyle relay. He was beaten on points in the middleweight boxing final by Britain's John Douglas, yet in a rematch a few days after the Olympics, he knocked out Douglas. In later years, Baker starred in silent films, then moved to Hollywood and taught fencing, riding and swimming to stars such as Greta Garbo, Douglas Fairbanks, Shirley Temple, Rudolph Valentino and Elizabeth Taylor.

Australia's senior IOC member is Kevan Gosper. Gosper was a very good quarter-miler on the track and won the national 440-yard title five times in succession. In 1956, as a member of the Australian 4 x 400-metre relay, he won an Olympic silver medal.

THE INTERNATIONAL OLYMPIC COMMITTEE

The International Olympic Committee, or IOC, is the body which is responsible for governing the Olympic Games. It was established by the founder of the modern Games, Baron Pierre de Coubertin, and the members of this august body are selected by the committee itself. They do not represent individual countries and are expected to be free from political, national and commercial influences.

Generally there is only one member from any one country but the exception is for those countries which have hosted an Olympic Games. Australia has two IOC delegates: Kevan Gosper, who competed at two Games as a runner, and Phil Coles, a former kayaker.

IOC members are elected for life but there is a compulsory retiring age of seventy-two.

Throughout the whole 100-year history of the International Olympic Committee, there have only been seven presidents. Apart from de Coubertin's early authority, perhaps the man who exerted the strongest influence on the Olympic movement was Avery Brundage.

Brundage was president from 1952 to 1972 and was uncompromising in his belief of the amateur ideal and sought to keep the Games 'pure'. While many believe the Games have now gone down the path of commercialism, it was Brundage who kept the real Olympic spirit alive for all those years.

The present president of the IOC is Juan Antonio Samaranch.

> Leonard Cuff became Australasia's first IOC member back in 1894, two years before the first Games of the modern era.

BOB BEAMON

The 1968 Olympic Games were held in the rarefied air of Mexico City. Prior to the Games, very little was know about the prospects of competing at altitude. However, it was known that those taking part in an explosive event like the long jump would be aided.

The field for the long jump included all three medallists from the previous Games—Lynn Davies from Britain, Ralph Boston of the USA and Russia's Igor Ter-Ovanesyan. But the favourite was a 22-year-old from New York, Bob Beamon.

On his very first attempt, Beamon had the perfect jump. He sailed through the air and landed in the pit to record a bewildering distance of 8.90 metres. In the old measurement, this was 29 feet $2^1/_2$ inches, a staggering $21^3/_4$ inches further than anyone had ever jumped. Defending champion Davies turned to Beamon and told him: 'You have just destroyed this event.'

Beamon sank to the ground and experienced what doctors called a 'cataplectic seizure', which comes to an individual following a period of great emotional excitement.

The dashing young star's feat was immediately hailed as the greatest athletic achievement of all time. Many experts said the record might never be broken.

Well, almost twenty-three years later, Mike Powell finally eclipsed the fabled mark when he soared to 8.95 metres or 29 feet $4^1/_2$ inches.

> The man who lit the flame at the Opening Ceremony of the Tokyo Olympics in 1964 was Japanese student Yoshinori Sakai. He was born on the day the atomic bomb was dropped on Hiroshima.

JON SIEBEN

The hot favourite for the 200-metre butterfly at the 1984 Los Angeles Olympics was the great German swimmer Michael Gross.

It was expected that Gross, the world record holder, would win the event and the minor placings would be fought out between Pablo Morales of the United States and Rafael Vidal from Venezuela. However, over in lane six was a young Australian—Jon Sieben.

Sieben had arrived in Los Angeles a virtual unknown. He had picked up a gold medal at the Commonwealth Games in Brisbane two years previously but this was as a member of the medley relay team. Few people, except for the Australians, paid any attention to him.

After the first lap of the race Sieben was in sixth position and improved this to fifth at the halfway mark. But all 200-metre races are won in the third lap! This is where he made his move and before the 150-metre mark he had surged past Vidal.

At thirty metres to go, the boy from Brisbane caught the front-runner Gross and with the next few strokes took the lead. When Sieben touched the wall he found he had not only won the event but had swum the amazing time of 1 minute 57.04 seconds, a new world record.

Jon Sieben was coached by the eccentric Laurie Lawrence and to say Laurie reacted with enthusiasm after the race would be an understatement. By his own admission he 'went out of my tree'. At the end of the victory ceremony it was difficult to tell who was more excited, the coach or the swimmer.

Following the Games, Sieben returned to a hero's welcome. While some of Australia's other gold medallists from Los Angeles had been favoured by the Eastern Bloc boycott, Sieben had taken on the very best in the world and walked away with sport's most treasured prize. His victory was truly a great one!

> The modern Olympics became a reality on 6 April 1896, when at 3 00 p.m., King George I of Greece pronounced the following words: 'I declare the opening of the first international Olympic Games in Athens.' Thus after an absence of some 1500 years, the greatest sporting festival in the world was again being celebrated.

1972 BASKETBALL FINAL

One of the greatest games of basketball took place in the final of the Olympic competition at the Munich Games of 1972. The combatants were the USA and the Soviet Union.

The United States came into this match with a perfect record. Throughout the whole period of the modern Games, the USA had never lost a match. They had the extraordinary Olympic statistics of sixty-two wins and no losses.

The game started at 11.45 p.m. in order to cater for American television.

Throughout the match the Soviets held the lead but with just six seconds left the USA had clawed their way back to be within striking distance. They were behind by a mere point.

American Doug Collins was then fouled. He walked to the free throw line and sank two shots to give the US its first lead in the game, 50–49. The time-out horn sounded just as Collins released his second shot and, after much arguing among officials, the time clock was set back to three seconds. In that short space of time, Russia's Sasha Belov pushed past two defenders and scored the winning basket.

The US filed an unsuccessful protest. They refused to accept their silver medals. Their coach, Hank Iba, felt doubly robbed for while he was signing the official protest, he had his pocket picked of $370.

> When Herb Elliott won the 1500 metres at the Rome Olympics his time was good enough to have lapped Australia's only other 1500-metre winner, Edwin Flack. Flack won in 1896.

JOHN DEVITT

These days, John Devitt is best known in Australian sporting circles as a vice-president of the Australian Olympic Committee. But in the late 1950s and early 1960s he was part of Australia's Golden Era of Swimming.

Devitt had competed at the 1956 Melbourne Games and finished second to fellow Australian Jon Henricks in the 'blue ribbon' event, the 100-metre freestyle. He had also secured a gold as a member of the 4 × 200-metre relay team.

By the time the Rome Olympics of 1960 had rolled around Devitt was the world record holder for the 100 metres. He also had three gold medals from the 1958 Empire Games in his bag.

The final of the 100 metres in Rome produced one of the most controversial finishes in Olympic history. With thirty metres to go, Dos Santos from Brazil was in the lead. Both Devitt and the American Lance Larson stormed home and the finish was extremely close. Two of the three first-place judges had Devitt as the winner but two of the three second-place judges had him second.

The timekeepers clocked Larson in a faster time. They recorded the American at 55.1 seconds while Devitt's time was 55.2 seconds. The race verdict went to Devitt on the fact that two of the three first-place judges placed the Australian first. The chief judge did not cast a vote on the finish. Both swimmers were given a time of 55.2 seconds, in keeping with FINA rules.

The Americans protested the results. The decision remained but the Americans raised the matter for a further six years.

There are arguments even today as to who won but there was one possibility not given due consideration at the time—was Devitt's time correct? Many on the finish line and in the stands clocked the Australian at a sub 55 seconds and thought he won.

Perhaps the important point to come from the controversy was the accelerated development of electronic timing for international competition. Now, with the advent of video cameras, all doubt is removed.

> The boycott over the 1984 Los Angeles Games by Eastern Bloc countries played havoc with the sport of weightlifting. Ninety-four of the world's top 100 ranked lifters were absent as were twenty-nine of the thirty medallists from the previous world championships.

DANIELLE WOODWARD

Danielle Woodward, a Victorian Federal policewoman and slalom canoeist, had only a remote chance of competing in the 1992 Barcelona Olympics. Her chances had taken a dive during the 1990 world championships when she severely injured her shoulder and was forced to take six months off training. When the Olympic qualifying trials were held in Europe in 1991, she was restricted in her preparation and was not included when the Australian team was announced. However she was allowed the opportunity to prove herself in competition over the ensuing months and eventually was added to the team. It proved a wise move. Danielle won a silver medal to take Australia's first-ever slalom canoeing medal in Olympic competition.

> Women were banned from competing in the ancient Olympic Games. And, under pain of death, they were not even allowed to view the competitions. Eventually women held their own Games and they were dedicated to the goddess Hera.

ANDREW 'BOY' CHARLTON

Andrew 'Boy' Charlton is one of Australia's greatest sporting heroes. He competed in three Olympic Games and featured in some of the classic swimming confrontations of the 1920s.

On the way to his first Games in Paris, in 1924, Charlton's coach, Tom Adrian, suffered a nervous breakdown and threw himself off the ship. He was fished out safely but many feared that Charlton's performances would be affected by the experience.

This was not to be! Instead, the Manly teenager was steeled by the incident and easily won the 1500-metre freestyle event from the famous Swedish swimmer Arne Borg. He also broke Borg's two-day-old world record by more than a minute.

In the 400-metre event, Charlton came up against America's Johnny Weissmuller, later to become the most famous of all the Hollywood Tarzans. Weissmuller won the race and the Swede, Borg, finished second. Charlton took out the bronze medal.

Four years later in Amsterdam, Borg was ready for Charlton and won the 1500 metres. In the 400-metre freestyle these two were so intent on their personal duel they allowed the Argentinean Alberto Zorrilla to sneak by and he beat them both.

Following the 1928 Games, the Boy announced his retirement. Enticed back into the pool, he went to his third Olympics in Los Angeles in 1932 but was overweight and suffered from an attack of influenza. He was unplaced in the 400-metre final.

Andrew Boy Charlton was inducted into the International Swimming Hall of Fame in 1972 and in January 1995 was honoured as a legend of Australian swimming at the official opening of the Sydney International Aquatic Centre. The Sydney Domain Baths are named after this immortal of Australian sport.

ANTHROPOLOGY DAYS

One of the greatest blemishes on the modern Olympic Games was the so-called 'Anthropology Days' at the St Louis Games of 1904.

The organisers of these Games decided to hold sports competitions for some of the world's 'primitive' peoples as part of the Exposition. Athletic contests were held among Pygmies and Kaffirs of Africa; the Ainus from Japan; Patagonians from South America; Moros and Ingorots from the Philippines; 'Red' Indians and Chinese.

A Patagonian won the shot-put; the Pygmies took out the mud fight and a Sioux Indian won the 100-yard dash. There was even a boxing event for women.

The whole concept of Anthropology Days was a sad chapter in the Olympic movement.

Bill Northam, who skippered the 32 foot sloop *Barrenjoey* to victory at the Tokyo Games of 1964, was knighted for his efforts in the New Year's Honours List of 1977. Northam won his gold at the ripe old age of fifty-nine.

MELBOURNE OLYMPICS

In 1956 the Olympic Games were staged in the Southern Hemisphere for the first time when Melbourne played host to the world's biggest sporting competition. However, because Australia was so distant from most other countries and the world was not the 'global village' we know today, the number of competitors taking part was the smallest since 1932.

Australia's strict quarantine laws also caused the Games to be split for the first time ever. The equestrian events were held separately in Stockholm, a situation the International Olympic Committee said would never happen again.

The Melbourne Games were also marred by boycotts. Several Middle Eastern countries withdrew over the Israeli-led takeover of the Suez Canal while Holland, Spain and Switzerland boycotted over the Soviet invasion of Hungary.

Melbourne also saw an innovation at the Closing Ceremony. Following a suggestion by John Wing, an Australian-born Chinese, it was decided to let all the athletes march together as a symbol of global unity. This practice was continued for a number of Games. However, more recently it has been substituted by only the flag-bearers marching intermingled. At the conclusion of the formal section of the ceremony, all the athletes are then invited onto the arena and what usually follows is a wild, carefree occasion marking the end of the Games.

> The Australian Olympic Federation changed its constitution, and its name, in 1990. What was previously the AOF became the AOC, the Australian Olympic Committee.

PARAPLEGIC ARCHER

If you search through the results of the archery competition from the 1984 Los Angeles Olympic Games you will not find the name of Neroli Fairhall in the medal table. She finished thirty-fifth in the women's individual event. Yet this young woman from New Zealand received much of the applause at the finish of the contest.

Fairhall had established an Olympic record of her own. She had become the first paraplegic athlete to take part in the Olympic Games. Paralysed from the waist down following a motorbike accident, she competed while seated in a wheelchair.

Rowing gold medallist Merv Wood is the only Australian to have ever been given the honour of carrying Australia's flag at two Olympic Games. He led the team into the stadium in Helsinki in 1952 and performed the same duty, before his home crowd in Melbourne four years later.

KORNELIA ENDER

In the 1970s the East German women ruled supreme in the swimming pool. One in particular stood out: Kornelia Ender.

Ender was born on 25 October 1958 in the town of Plauen and took up swimming at the age of ten on the advice of her doctor. She had a deviated hip bone and the doctor thought the water sport would be good therapy for her.

Before her fourteenth birthday Ender had swum in her first Olympics, at the Munich Games of 1972. She won three silver medals, two in relays.

In 1973 she began breaking world records and in 1974 took home four gold medals from the European Championships. The following year, at the World Championships, she won four more gold medals plus a silver.

Then came the Montreal Olympics. This time she again scored her almost customary four gold medals and a silver. Two of these events, the 200-metre freestyle and the 100-metre butterfly, were held within twenty-five minutes of each other. She set a world record in one and equalled it in the other.

By this time Kornelia Ender had set twenty-three world records, in all strokes except backstroke. Perhaps this is why she ended up marrying the other famous East German swimmer of this period, the great Roland Matthes. Matthes was a backstroker.

Ender was a powerfully built swimmer and many referred to her as a swimming machine. But she had plenty of other interests and retired just after her eighteenth birthday to continue her studies.

> **B**ritain's women high jumpers finished second in every Olympics from 1936 to 1960.

DAWN FRASER

Without doubt, Dawn Fraser is Australia's best-known and much-loved Olympian. She won four gold medals at three Games and her record of winning the 100-metre freestyle at three consecutive Olympics will probably never be beaten, or equalled, by any Australian athlete.

Dawn started her Olympic career at the Melbourne Games of 1956. At those Olympics she was part of our marvellous swim team which dominated the pool. Not only did she win the 100 in world record time (62.0 seconds), she also took out a second gold as a member of the 4 x 100-metre freestyle and a silver, finishing second behind Lorraine Crapp in the 400 metres.

Four years later Dawn went to Rome and at those Games in the Eternal City she repeated her 100 win and took out two more silver medals in the form of two relays.

It was between 1960 and 1964 that Dawn Fraser really left her mark on world swimming. First, in 1962 she became the first woman to break the magic minute for 110 yards and then, at the 1964 Olympic trials, she registered a time of 58.9 seconds for 100 metres. In that same period she managed to win four gold medals at the Perth Commonwealth Games in 1962.

Dawn was selected for her third Olympics in 1964. She again took out the 100-metre title and won her eighth Olympic medal when the Australian women's freestyle relay team finished second.

But it was in Tokyo that she incurred the ire of the Australian Swimming Union. She had been involved in several 'incidents' at the time of the Games and ASU officials were not impressed. One of these incidents was the 'souveniring' of a flag from the Emperor's Palace. Then there was her insistence on marching in the Opening Ceremony after being specifically forbidden to do so.

Back home in Australia she was barred from swimming for life, however this ban was replaced with a ten-year restraint. The ban was eventually lifted after four years but it effectively ended the great champion's career. Had this girl from Balmain been allowed to compete at the Mexico City Olympics in 1968, there is little doubt she would have won the 100 at those Games also. But such was not to be.

Dawn Fraser stands tall on the global Olympic stage and at the Atlanta Games she was honoured by the International Olympic Committee as being one of the true 'greats' of the Olympic movement.

Following on from Edwin Flack's successes at the first Games at Athens in 1896 it was reported in a Melbourne newspaper that the Olympic Games... 'may in due course offer themselves to the delighted gaze of Melbourne'. Very prophetic words as the Games came to our southern capital some sixty years later.

1988 BOXING UPSETS

At the 1988 Seoul Olympics, the local favourite for the light flyweight boxing gold medal, Oh Kwang-soo, was narrowly upset by an American rival. The next day another Korean, bantamweight Byun Jong-il, lost a brawling encounter to a Bulgarian after the referee deducted points for head butting. That was too much for the Koreans! A trainer jumped into the ring and struck the referee on the back. Others followed and within seconds the ring was filled with angry Koreans pummelling the New Zealand ref, Keith Walker. He had to be escorted from the ring but not before some of the Korean security guards also lashed out at him. After the ring was cleared, the beaten fighter sat down in the middle in a silent 67-minute protest. Meantime, the referee went straight to his hotel, checked out, and took the next flight home.

The finish of the marathon in 1948 provided quite a spectacle. Etienne Gally, a Belgian war veteran, entered the stadium first but was so physically exhausted he was overtaken on the last lap by Delfo Cabrera from Argentina.

DON SCHOLLANDER

Before Mark Spitz's feats at the 1972 Munich Games, the most celebrated American Olympic swimming champion was Don Schollander. At the Tokyo Olympics in 1964 Schollander became the first swimmer in history to win four gold medals in a single Olympiad.

Schollander came from the very powerful Santa Clara swim club in California. He was noted for both his speed through the water and the style and perfection of his stroke. He first started breaking world records in the early 1960s and in 1963 he became the first person to swim 200 metres in less than two minutes. In fact between July 1963 and August 1968 he improved the time for this distance a total of nine times.

In Tokyo, the blond, good-looking youngster won both the 100-metre and 400-metre freestyle events, the latter in world record time. His other two golds came as a member of the 400-metre and 800-metre relay teams.

When the Mexico City Olympics rolled round, it was anticipated Schollander would not only repeat in the two individual events he won four years previously, but also take out the 200 metres which had been added to the Olympic program for the first time. But he didn't count on an Australian named Mike Wenden.

Wenden surprised all and took out the sprint double (100 and 200). The American hero could only manage a silver for any of the individual events.

If Spitz had not come along, it is quite possible the name of Don Schollander would be up there in lights, in the eyes of the American public, just as Jesse Owens is today.

> Between the years of 1948 and 1960 Sweden's Gert Fredriksson won an incredible six golds, a silver and a bronze. No wonder he was known as the King of Olympic Canoeing.

HAROLD ABRAHAMS

Due to the 1981 movie *Chariots of Fire*, most of the world now knows the name of Harold Abrahams. He was one of the two central characters in this wonderful movie, set around the 1924 Paris Olympics.

Abrahams had been born into an athletic family. His brother Sidney had represented Great Britain in the 1912 Games and Harold himself had participated in the Games following the First World War, the Antwerp competition of 1920.

Between 1920 and 1924 Abrahams competed for Cambridge University and won a number of sprint and long jump events. He trained under Sam Mussabini, another character featured prominently in the David Puttnam movie.

At the 1924 Olympics, Abrahams defeated the American favourites, Jackson Scholz and Charley Paddock, in the 100-metre event. His main British rival was Eric Liddell who did not compete because the race was held on a Sunday. Liddell was a devout Christian but contrary to popular myth, he never had any intention of running in the sprint. He had set his sights on the 400 metres and this he won.

Harold Abrahams suffered an injury the year following the Paris Olympics and never competed again. He became a radio broadcaster of some repute and went into the administration of the British Amateur Athletics Association. He also wrote about athletics and authored a number of books including *The Olympic Games, 1896–1952*.

> Dawn Fraser held the world record for 100 metres freestyle from 1956 until 1972. The person who took it away from her was Shane Gould!

DICK FOSBURY

Up until the late 1960s most high jumpers around the world used a style called the straddle-roll. But then along came an American called Dick Fosbury.

Fosbury found the straddle-roll jumping style complicated and had trouble with it while competing in high school track meets. So he began to develop his own style which featured a backward 'flop' action. Initially, he was discouraged by his coach from using this method but when the youngster started to produce results, there was no reason for him not to continue it.

The 'Fosbury Flop', as it soon became known, consisted of the jumper running up at great speed, taking off on the left foot, pivoting the right leg and approaching the bar, head first, with the back to the bar.

Dick Fosbury made his international debut at the Mexico City Games. Most of the athletes and coaches who first saw the lanky American warming up said he would never make it past the preliminaries. But they were proved wrong. Fosbury went on to win the event by more than an inch and in doing so set a new Olympic record. The Fosbury Flop had arrived.

Nowadays, nearly every jumper in the world uses this style.

At the first Olympic Games in 1896 there were only thirteen nations which had official representation. One hundred years later in Atlanta, 197 nations marched into the main arena for the Opening Ceremony.

LIONEL COX

Lionel Cox is the proud possessor of two Olympic medals, both won at the Helsinki Games of 1952. In the 1000-metre sprint he picked up a silver and, teaming up with Russell Mockridge, he won gold in the now discontinued tandem event.

But prior to arriving in the Finnish capital the Sydney cyclist had hardly ever seen a tandem and certainly had never straddled one.

Mockridge had been given the bike in London by an English manufacturer. It had been rejected by the British team. He brought it to Helsinki and suggested to Cox, the only other track bikie on the Australian team, that they enter the 2000-metre race.

After surviving a brief scare in their race against the Danes the pair made it through to the finals and eventually beat the South Africans for the gold medal.

On that same day, Cox also raced in the sprint final and whether or not it was the exuberance of having won a gold medal, or poor tactics, he could only manage a second.

Not a bad effort, however, a gold and a silver in one day.

Jackie Robinson was the first black to compete in major league baseball in America. His brother Mathew or 'Mack', finished second to the celebrated Jesse Owens in the 200 metres at the Berlin Olympics of 1936.

JUDO IN JAPANESE GAMES

When judo was introduced into the Olympics at the Tokyo Games of 1964, it was assumed that the Japanese would have a clean sweep of the gold medals. They did very well in most of the various classes but in the open event, along came a Dutchman named Antonius Geesink who upset the applecart.

Geesink's victory was a great blow to the Japanese even though he had won the world championship twice. In 1961, the gentle giant from Utrecht became the first non-Japanese to win the world title and, on paper, was the favourite for the Olympic crown.

In the semi-final he beat Australia's Theo Boronovskis in one of the fastest fights of the tournament. It lasted only twelve seconds.

The final pitted Geesink against Akio Kaminaga. Despite the very vocal support from the crowd for the local hero, the 121-kilo Hollander won the bout and took home the prized gold.

Interestingly, Boronovskis finished third in the division and won a bronze medal. It is our only judo medal in Olympic competition.

It's no wonder the Olympic Games have a somewhat regal association. The first Games of 1896 had the total support of the King of Belgium, Britain's Prince of Wales, the Crown Prince of Sweden and the Crown Prince of Greece.

FIRST MEDAL FOR CHINA

Traditionally, the first gold medal at any Olympic Games goes to the winner of a shooting event. In 1984 it went to the winner of the free pistol event.

However, this winner created history for another reason. His name was Xu Haifeng and he came from China, and in 1984 China was competing at its first Olympics. Being the first winner at those Games, Xu became the first representative of that country to win any Olympic medal.

The Chinese propagandists really pumped up the publicity hype with this win and claimed Xu was a former 'barefoot doctor' who now worked as a fertiliser salesman. An interesting combination!

> Michel Theato of France won the marathon in his home town of Paris in 1900 because he had local knowledge of the course acquired through work. Theato was a baker's roundsman and delivered bread around the city every day.

POLISH FENCER

In Europe, most elite fencers come from the privileged class. But in the Eastern Bloc countries, many emerge from the military ranks.

Jerzy Pawlowski was a major in the Polish Army. He had received his master's degree in law having written his dissertation on 'A Critique of Hayek's Neo-Liberal Conception of Liberty and Law'. Heavy stuff!

Jerzy Pawlowski was also a fencer—a sabre fencer—and by the time of the Mexico City Olympics already had three world titles under his belt. At the 1968 Games he beat the Russian Rakita to take out the gold.

In the military arena, Pawlowski was considered a protégé of General Jaruzelski who later became Premier of Poland. In 1981 the Olympic champion was asked by his government to become a spy. When he refused, he was charged with *being* a spy and sentenced to twenty-five years in prison. All mention of him in Polish books about the Olympics was deleted.

It would be interesting to know in the light of the recent détente whether or not Pawlowski had been returned to his former status.

When New Zealand's Peter Snell won the 800- and 1500-metre double at the Tokyo Games of 1964, it was not the first time this feat had been accomplished. Albert Hill of Great Britain had won the same two events in 1920.

YOUNGEST AND OLDEST GOLD IN ROWING

The youngest gold medallist in Olympic history is believed to be the French boy who coxed the Dutch pairs to victory in 1900. Unfortunately the name of this youngster is unknown but it has been established he was between seven and ten years of age. The original cox had been Hermanus Brockmann but following the heats he was replaced as he was considered to be too heavy.

Incidentally, Brockmann had some success at those first Paris Games as a cox with other teams. He guided the Dutch fours to a silver medal and the eights to a bronze.

A number of other coxswains have been very young. Another French boy, Noel Vandernotte, was aged twelve years and 233 days when he won bronze medals at the 1936 Games with the French pairs and fours. The latter team included his father and his uncle.

At the other end of the scale is Robert Zimonyi. In 1964 he was cox of the American eights when he was forty-six years and 180 days. That team won the gold medal and made Zimonyi the oldest ever gold medallist in rowing.

The oldest oarsman to win a gold medal was Guy Nickalls from Britain who was a member of their eights in 1908. He was forty-two years and 170 days.

> At the Montreal Games of 1976 Finland's Lasse Viren set a remarkable record when he became the first man ever to win both the 5000- and 10,000-metre track events in successive Olympics.

SPORTSMANSHIP IN CYCLING

One of the finest acts of sportsmanship in Olympic competition took place at the first modern Games in Athens. The year was 1896 and the event was the 100-kilometre track race.

The race involved only two competitors, Leon Flameng from France and Greece's Georgios Kolettis. It was ridden on a 333.33-metre circular track and thus required the riders to complete 300 laps.

Well into the race, Flameng was leading when the Greek's bike broke down and needed to be repaired. Flameng stopped and waited until it was replaced and then continued.

Towards the end of the race the Frenchman took a tumble but he got up and continued, still winning by six or seven laps. He raced with the French tricolour tied around his leg.

At the other end of the scale we have the worst in sportsmanship, also in cycling.

In 1936, another Frenchman, Robert Charpentier, beat his team-mate Guy Lapebie by 0.2 second at the end of the 100-kilometre road race. Inexplicably, the latter had been leading but slowed down just before the line. It was later discovered, in a photograph of the finish, that Charpentier had pulled Lapebie back by his shirt.

Apparently one gold was not enough for Charpentier. Two days previously he had won a gold as a member of the victorious team pursuit.

> Avery Brundage, the Chicago millionaire who became president of the IOC in 1952, was known as 'Slavery Bondage' for his strict adherence to the amateur rules.

FIRST WEIGHTLIFTING GOLD

At the first Olympic Games of the modern era, at Athens in 1896, there were two weightlifting events. The first was the two-handed lift and the second was the one-hand lift.

In the latter event Launceston Elliot became Britain's first Olympic champion when he lifted 71 kilos, much more than the Dane Viggo Jensen, who could only manage 57.2 kilos. However, in the two-hand event the order was reversed. Both lifters had raised the same weight, 111.5 kilos, but Jensen was awarded the gold because of his better style. Elliot had moved one foot while lifting.

There was an interesting aside to the first weightlifting competition. An attendant was having considerable trouble moving one of the weights. Prince George of Greece, who was on the organising committee and a very big and strong man, reached down and easily moved it.

Viggo Jensen was quite an athlete. As well as his successes in weightlifting he came away from Athens with a second in the free pistol competition and a third in the military rifle event. He also finished fourth in the rope climb.

> Mexico City, 1968, saw two major landmarks in the sport of track and field. The world of high jumping was introduced to a new style when Dick Fosbury came along and used the 'Fosbury Flop' and Bob Beamon jumped out of his skin in the long jump when he went a distance of 29 feet 2½ inches.

KIEREN PERKINS

If Edwin Flack, Australia's first Olympic gold medallist from the 1896 Games in Athens, is known as the Lion of Athens, then Kieren Perkins, the winner of the 1500-metre freestyle at both Barcelona and Atlanta, should go down in history as the Lazarus of Atlanta.

Kieren burst onto the international scene when he was narrowly defeated by the German Jorg Hoffman in the 1500-metre freestyle at the world championships of 1991. But from that swim, the world knew there was something special ahead for this young, good-looking Queenslander.

The following year, at the Barcelona Olympics, Perkins swept all before him in the 1500 and won by over twenty metres in the new Olympic and world time of 14 minutes 43.48 seconds. He was also second to the Russian Yevgeni Sadovyi in the 400 metres.

The year 1994 was a great one for Perkins. He won the 400 and 1500 at both the Commonwealth Games and the World Championships, and along the way created new world marks for his pet distances. But it was in Atlanta, at the Games of the twenty-sixth Olympiad, that Perkins established himself as a great champion.

Kieren just made the Olympic team at the Australian trials in April. He finished second to his old sparring mate Daniel Kowalski in the 1500. In Atlanta, he barely made it into the final, qualifying in lane eight, and no-one gave him a chance. However, Perkins showed in that event that he should never be underestimated.

Realising that the water in lane eight was exactly the same as the water in lane four, he took on all his competitors and after thirty gruelling laps, which he later admitted were 'the hardest I have ever done', he emerged as the Olympic champion.

It was one of the greatest comebacks in sporting history.

1992 SHOT-PUT FAVOURITE

Overwhelming shot-put favourite at the Barcelona Olympics was Sweden's Werner Gunthor. But a couple of weeks before the Olympics, a German magazine published drug allegations, trying to make hay out of admissions from a doctor years before that the thrower had been given a kind of steroid to help overcome an injury. The media drove Gunthor mad asking about the story. Then, on his way to the final, the fifteen-minute trip from the village to the main stadium, turned into an hour-long nightmare when the bus driver got lost. Gunthor went straight into the competition without warming up and, as a result, only came fourth. US winner Mike Stuce said, 'Going into this competition, we all felt we were jockeying for second place, since no-one felt Gunthor could be beat.'

At the Berlin Olympics of 1936 the voice of Pierre de Coubertin was played over the loudspeakers at the Opening Ceremony. At that stage, the founder of the modern Games was a very old man and died the following year.

THE OLYMPIC TRUCE

One of the unique features of the ancient Games was the Olympic truce.

The word truce, in Greek, is *ekecheiria* which literally means 'holding of hands'. It was announced before each of the Olympic festivals and it allowed visitors to travel in safety to the site of the Games at Olympia.

During the truce period, all wars were suspended and the carrying out of death penalties was forbidden. Armies were also prohibited from entering that region of Greece known as Elis, on the Peloponnese. It was here that the sacred grove, dedicated to Zeus, was located.

For the most part, the truce was observed, however the famous historian Thucydides does record one violation. In his writings he recounts how the Lacedaemonians attacked the fortress at Lepreum, in Elis, during one of the Olympic truces. Because of this, they were banned from taking part in the Games and were fined by the Eleans.

The truce of Olympia not only allowed worshippers and athletes to travel freely, they also provided a common basis for peace among the Greeks. It is a pity the Olympic truce is not a feature of the modern Olympics.

When Japan staged the first Asian Olympics in 1964, they set new standards for architectural design of competition facilities. The aquatic complex was akin to a temple to swimming and the main stadium was declared one of the best in the world.

AVERY BRUNDAGE

The man who did more than anyone to shape the Olympic Games as we know them today was Avery Brundage.

Brundage started his association with the Olympic movement back in 1912 when he represented his native America at the Stockholm Games. He was a track and field athlete and took part in the pentathlon and decathlon. While he failed to finish in the latter competition he did manage a creditable sixth in the five-discipline event. The great American Indian Jim Thorpe won both these golds only to see his medals taken away from him after being declared a professional. (In 1982 the International Olympic Committee reversed this decision and the medals were returned to Thorpe's family the following year.)

Shortly after finishing his active career, Brundage founded his own construction company and it grew and grew. Eventually, he was a multimillionaire. But his interest in amateur sport never left him.

In 1928 Brundage was elected to the all-powerful presidency of the Amateur Athletic Union and the following year he was made president of the US Olympic Committee. He served in this role until 1953. In 1936 he was elected to the IOC, the 'Lords of the Rings', and eventually became president of that body in 1952. He remained at the reins until 1972.

Brundage was convinced that amateur competition was the only way to go for the Olympics. He considered amateurs to be the 'purist' of athletes and threatened or punished those who contravened his rules, even for minor infractions.

This colossus and domineering force on the world's sport stage also saw political events as being totally unrelated to Olympic competition. He refused to boycott Hitler's Games of 1936 and insisted the Munich Games 'must go on' after the murder of eleven Israeli athletes. He died in 1975.

LENI RIEFENSTAHL—
OLYMPIC FILMMAKER

When people talk about films that were made on or about the Olympic Games, they always come back to the movie made at the 1936 Berlin games, *Olympia*. This movie is a classic and it was made by Hitler's favourite cinematographer, Leni Riefenstahl.

Riefenstahl was born in 1902 and started her career as first a ballet dancer and then, an actress. By the early 1930s she had turned her hand to directing and soon became the top film executive of the Nazi Party. She made several movies on the so-called 'national renaissance' which culminated in the powerful Nuremberg rally film, *Triumph of the Will*. Over 100 people worked on this film and in excess of thirty cameras were used to capture 'everything that moved' at this rally.

This type of saturation coverage was again employed by Riefenstahl when she was commissioned to make the official film of the 1936 Games. What resulted was a classic documentary, of four hours duration, released in two parts. It had its premiere on 20 April 1938, to mark Adolf Hitler's birthday.

Olympia, with its technical innovation and devotion to the athletic, muscular form, was awarded first prize at the Venice Biennale and the IOC gave the director a special award in 1948. Many cinema buffs consider Riefenstahl's Olympic film to be one of the top ten movies of all time.

> Australia competed for the first time at the Winter Games at Garmisch-Partenkirchen in Germany. The year was 1936.

ROLAND MATTHES

The dominant swimmer in the backstroke discipline during the late 1960s and early 1970s was East Germany's Roland Matthes. In that time he set sixteen world records and collected an amazing eight Olympic medals.

At the Mexico City Games of 1968, Matthes won both the 100-metre and 200-metre titles, as well as a silver medal as a member of his country's medley relay team. Four years later in Munich, he repeated this effort and added a bronze medal in the 4 ×100-metre relay.

Matthes looked very casual moving through the water but this was because all his effort was being put into the long follow-through stroke under the surface.

In six years, this East German 'freak' took the world record for the 100-metre event down from 58.4 seconds to 56.3 seconds. His improvement of the 200-metre mark is perhaps more dramatic. In that same space of time he lowered the mark from 2 minutes 07.9 seconds to 2 minutes 01.87 seconds, an astonishing six seconds.

Matthes went to the 1976 Games in Montreal, but by then his heart was not really in swimming. He won only a bronze medal in the 100-metre event.

Following those Games he retired and married a teammate and fellow 'superstar', Kornelia Ender. Unfortunately, that marriage broke up in the late 1980s.

> Australia competed as an independent country for the first time at the Antwerp Games of 1920. Australia competed with New Zealand under the name Australasia at the 1908 and 1912 Olympics. Before this Australians competed individually.

ZOLTAN HALMAY

One of the most controversial swimming races in Olympic history took place at the third Games of the modern era. It was the 50-yard freestyle event held at St Louis in 1904.

The two favourites were Zoltan Halmay of Hungary and America's Scott Leary. At the end of the one-lap dash, Halmay had clearly defeated Leary by a foot, however the US judge awarded the race to Leary. A brawl broke out and after some time it was decided to call the race a dead heat with the two men asked to swim-off.

After two false starts, the race got under way and this time Halmay clearly won. His time was given as 28.0 seconds with Leary credited with 28.6 seconds.

The Hungarian featured in the medals at four Olympic Games. In 1900, he finished second to Australia's Freddie Lane in the 200-metre event. Then in 1904, 1906 (the Intercalated Games in Athens), and 1908, he was among the placings in the 100-metre event.

Halmay swam exclusively with his arms. His stroke was devoid of any propulsion from the legs and he relied entirely on upper-body strength.

> When the majority of the Australian swimming team were banned from taking part in the Opening Ceremony at the Rome Games, they staged their own 'march' within the precinct of the Olympic village.

PAUL GONZALES

Paul Gonzales was raised in a Los Angeles ghetto. His father walked out on the family when he was seven leaving his mother to raise eight children. By the time he was nine, Gonzales had joined one of the gangs in his area. When he was 12, he was shot in the head when a car he was in stalled in a rival gang's territory. His cousin removed the shrapnel and glass with a pair of tweezers.

At fifteen he was arrested for murder but had a perfect alibi—he was boxing at the time and his coach was a policeman. That same policeman had convinced Gonzales to take up boxing after seeing him in a street fight. In the 1984 Olympic boxing ring, a few blocks from where he roamed in the gang, he became the Olympic light-flyweight champion. He also had this message: 'I won this not just for myself or my mom or my coach, but for the kids like me who are always told, "You're nothing…"'

In a most unusual double at the Moscow Olympics twin brothers Anatoly and Serhei Bilohlazov of the USSR competed in the freestyle wrestling competition—Anatoly in the flyweight division and Serhei in the bantamweight tournament. Both took out the gold medals!

BILLY MILLS

Going into the Tokyo Olympics of 1964, the strong favourite for the 10,000-metre run was Australia's Ron Clarke. He was the world record holder and had come a long way since lighting the flame at the cauldron in the Melbourne Cricket Ground to open the 1956 Games.

When the race started, there were several given a chance of knocking off the Australian but the name of Billy Mills was not one of them. Mills was a part Sioux Indian who grew up on an Indian reservation and was orphaned at the age of twelve. He joined the US Marine Corps and it was while he was serving with this body that he qualified for the American team to go to Tokyo.

By the halfway mark of the 10,000, Clarke had managed to shake off all potential challengers bar four: Africans Mohamed Gammoudi and Mamo Wolde, the local, Tsuburaya, and Billy Mills.

With a lap to go it was down to Gammoudi, Mills and Clarke and the Aussie must have felt confident as he was the only one of the three to have broken twenty-nine minutes. But the stragglers played havoc with the three of them. They all suffered one way or another but it was Mills who fought his way through, and with a final sprint crossed the line first.

The crowd of 75,000 went wild. He was surrounded by officials and journalists and one even asked him, 'Who are you?' In the whole period he had been in the Olympic city he had not once been approached by a journalist. Now he was an international celebrity.

Mills later confessed that he could not believe he had won. He said that the only person who thought he had a chance was himself.

In 1965, Mills was presented with a gold ring by the elders of the Oglala Sioux tribe and given an Indian name: Loves His Country. The 1983 film *Running Brave* was based on Billy Mills' Olympic victory.

While many nations boycotted the Moscow Games of 1980 because of the Afghanistan situation, Australia did send a team of 123 competitors. These athletes were led into the Lenin Stadium by dual flag-carriers Denise Boyd from track and field and Max Metzker from swimming. This was the only time dual flag-bearers have been used by Australia.

THE OPENING CEREMONY

The form of the ceremony at the opening of an Olympic Games is laid down in great detail by the International Olympic Committee.

It calls for the president of the IOC and the Organising Committee of the Games to meet the host country's Chief of State at the entrance of the stadium. They then move to the podium or tribune at which time the host nation's national anthem is played.

The parade of competitors then takes place. The Greek team is always the first to enter the arena and, except for the host team, which is always last, the other nations follow in alphabetical order. Each contingent is preceded with a plaque, bearing the name of its country, and an athlete carries its national flag. The competitors march around the stadium and then form up in the centre of the stadium, facing the podium.

Speeches then follow with the president of the Organising Committee welcoming one and all. He, or she, is then followed by the president of the IOC who makes a brief address and then asks the Chief of State to proclaim the Games open.

A fanfare of trumpets is sounded and the Olympic flag, which has been resident in the host city for the previous four years, then makes its appearance. It is carried around the stadium and finally hoisted over the arena to fly there until the Games are closed. Traditionally, pigeons are then released to spread the word to the countries of the world that the Games are now open.

One of the most eagerly awaited moments of the Opening Ceremony is the entrance of the Olympic flame. This flame has been carried to the host venue by a relay of runners from Olympia. The identity of the final runner is always kept a secret.

Over the past few Games several innovations have taken place in respect of this part of the ceremony.

In 1968, at Mexico City, a woman carried the flame into the stadium for the first time. Eight years later, the flame was borne jointly by a male and a female athlete. In Barcelona, the torch was lit by an archer. And in Atlanta, there was a relay of several well-known athletes culminating with the great Muhammad Ali lighting the torch.

> Marjorie Gestring was only thirteen years and nine months old when she won the springboard event in Berlin (1936). She remains the youngest person in Olympic history to win an individual gold medal in any sport.

OLYMPIC BOXING—FACTS AND FIGURES

The oldest boxer to win an Olympic gold medal was Richard Gunn of Great Britain. At the 1908 Games he took out the featherweight title when he was thirty-seven years and 254 days.

The youngest victor was Jackie Fields from the USA. Fields won at the second Paris Olympics in 1924, when he was sixteen years and 162 days and again it was the featherweight division.

The great Floyd Patterson won the 1952 middleweight gold when he was only seventeen years and 211 days. Four years later he became the youngest ever to win the world professional heavyweight crown.

A team-mate of Patterson's at the Helsinki Games (1952) was Norvel Lee. He had travelled to the Finnish capital as a reserve for the heavyweight class but at the last minute was entered in the light heavyweight competition. He had to lose over 6kg in a matter of days, however the weight reduction was richly rewarded. Not only did he take out the title but he was awarded a trophy for being the best boxer at the Games.

An interesting boxing story surrounds the Argentinean Santiago Lovell. Lovell won the heavyweight title in 1932 and when he arrived back home in Buenos Aires, he was met by the local police and taken to gaol. Apparently he had 'breached the peace' on the ship back home from Los Angeles.

> Two of the people to participate in the Olympic torch relay prior to the Los Angeles Games in 1984 were Bill Thorpe, the grandson of Jim Thorpe, and Gina Hemphill, grand daughter of Jesse Owens.

PAAVO NURMI—THE FLYING FINN

Whenever track and field athletes gather to discuss legends of their sport, one name that consistently comes to the fore is that of Paavo Nurmi, the Flying Finn. Nurmi won an incredible nine Olympic gold medals and if it had not been for a suspension by the ruling body of Athletics, the IAAF, he quite possibly would have won another two.

Nurmi's first Olympics were in Antwerp in 1920. He lost the final of the 5000 metres, to Frenchman Joseph Guillemot, but three days later took revenge in the 10,000 metres. At these same Games he won golds in the individual cross-country event and the teams cross-country. Over the next two Olympiads he picked up a further six gold medals.

In 1932 Nurmi had been considered the favourite to win the marathon but he was suspended one week before the race. The IAAF said he had accepted payments in excess of his expenses during an exhibition tour.

The great name of Paavo Nurmi surfaced again in 1952. When the athletes of the world gathered in the main stadium at the start of the Helsinki Games, they all waited to see who would bring the Olympic flame into the arena. When the runner emerged from a tunnel, the predominantly Finnish crowd broke into thunderous applause. It was Paavo Nurmi!

When the Flying Finn died in 1974, the whole nation wept. At his funeral no less than six Finnish gold medal winners acted as pallbearers.

Apart from his nine Olympic gold medals, Nurmi left a legacy of twenty-nine world records at distances ranging from 1500 metres to 20,000 metres.

GREAT SAILOR

The man considered to be the greatest sailor in Olympic history is the Dane Paul Elvstrom. Between 1948 and 1960 he dominated the Finn class, winning four consecutive gold medals.

Elvstrom was only twenty years old when he started his international yachting career at the London Games of 1948. Although getting off to a bad start—he failed to finish the first race of the series—he won the last two races and took out the coveted Olympic crown.

In earning his second gold medal at Helsinki, Elvstrom won four races and finished almost 3000 points ahead of his nearest rival. On Port Phillip Bay in 1956, he again won comfortably, taking the victory salute in the last four races. At the Rome Games, the yachting events were held on the Bay of Naples and once again the Olympic champion was Paul Elvstrom.

The sailor from Hellerup in Denmark retired after this fourth win but returned to Olympic competition in 1968. Unfortunately he did not win a medal.

In 1984 Paul Elvstrom sailed in the Tornado catamaran class with his daughter Trine and they narrowly missed the bronze medal. He competed in the Seoul Olympics with his other daughter Stine, but again did not win a medal.

> In the ancient Games, the distance of the first running races was a 'stade' or approximately 194 metres. From this word we have derived the name where athletic competitions are now held—the stadium.

FIRST SOUTH AFRICAN MEDALS IN 32 YEARS

When Wayne Ferreira and Piet Norval stood on the medal dais after taking out the silver medal for the doubles tennis tournament at the Barcelona Games of 1992, they became the first South Africans to win Olympic medals since their country was banned from Olympic competition after the 1960 Games. Their silver medals preceded another one by a South African athlete by less than five hours.

The athlete in question was Elana Meyer. She finished second behind Derartu Tulu of Ethiopia in the 10,000-metre event.

Following this race, one of the most touching sights in modern sport occurred. Tulu waited for Meyer to cross the line and then the two of them did a lap of honour, hand in hand.

Here was the first black African to win an Olympic gold medal, and a white South African, whose country had been banned from Olympic competition for thirty-two years because of their apartheid laws, showing the world that sport supersedes politics. A great sight!

In the teams parallel bars event at the first Games of 1896, the third placegetters were the gymnasts from the National Gymnastic Club of Athens. One of the members of this team was Dimitrios Loundras who was only ten years old. This event was held only once.

VLADIMIR SALNIKOV

Vladimir Salnikov of the Soviet Union is one of the greatest Olympians of all time. In all he won four gold medals and was the first person to swim the 1500 metres in less than fifteen minutes.

Salnikov won gold over his pet distance, the 1500, at both the Moscow and Seoul Olympics. Had it not been for his country's boycott in 1984, it is almost certain he would have won that year also. When he won in Seoul in 1988, he was twenty-eight years of age and he became the oldest swimmer in fifty-six years to win Olympic gold.

In 1980 this great Russian distance swimmer also won the 400-metre freestyle and was a member of his country's winning 4 x 200-metre relay team.

Vladimir Salnikov has been inducted into the International Swimming Hall of Fame.

The Olympic Games moved from Olympia to Rome in 146 BC. This occurred after the Roman occupation of Greece. By AD 394 the Christian forces ruling the Roman Empire called for a stop to all pagan festivals and thus the ancient Games came to an end.

STAMPS AND THE OLYMPIC GAMES

The first Olympic stamps were issued in early 1896 by the Greek Government to publicise the upcoming first modern Games. These stamps were also used as a form of revenue to help offset the mounting cost of staging the Games. The set consisted of designs of ancient boxers, the Olympic stadium and Myron's statue of the Discus Thrower. As many as four million copies of some of the smaller denominations were printed.

In 1920, for the Games in Antwerp, three stamps were issued. These depicted an ancient runner, a charioteer and once again, the Discus Thrower. Since this time there has always been a special commemorative issue of stamps by every host country.

In 1928 for the first time, representations of modern athletes were made on the set of eight stamps issued for the Amsterdam Games.

When Australia hosted the Games in 1956 the old Post Master General's Department produced six Olympic stamps for the Melbourne celebration. Following those Games, the Dominican Republic became the first country to issue stamps depicting the modern Olympic champions. In their set they had stamps with the likenesses of Al Oerter, Shirley Strickland and Ron Delaney featured.

Nowadays, nearly every country has an Olympic issue and they are used as an important publicity vehicle for the Olympic movement.

So popular was the sport of swimming with the citizens of Melbourne at the time of the 1956 Games that people waited in queues of up to 400 metres long just to see our team train.

MURRAY ROSE

The greatest Australian male Olympian of all time is Murray Rose. This is not simply a rash statement. The mantle was bestowed on Rose by a poll of his fellow Olympians in the early 1980s.

Iain Murray Rose burst onto the Olympic scene when, as a 17-year-old, he won three gold medals at the Melbourne Games of 1956. He was part of that magnificent Australian swim team that won every freestyle event in the pool.

In Melbourne Rose beat experienced swimmers such as Yamanaka from Japan and Breen of America in both the 400 metres and 1500 metres. These swims have gone down in the folklore of Australian sport and certainly have inspired many of the greats of distance swimming who have followed the blond champion.

Rose was also a member of the victorious 4 x 200-metre relay team which gave him his third gold.

In Rome four years later, Rose faced up to his old adversaries Yamanaka and Breen again but this time there was a new face on the scene—fellow Australian John Konrads. The wily Rose, who had spent the three previous years attending the University of Southern California, was successful in beating the trio over the 400 metres. But when it came to the 1500, Konrads, the world record holder, swam a perfect race and defeated the 'legend' by some three metres.

In 1964 the Australian Swimming Union had issued an edict stating that to make the team for the Tokyo Games a swimmer had to compete in trials in Australia. Rose was still living in America at this stage and did not turn up for the trials thus forfeiting his place on the team. This was a great pity as he swam several world records in North America prior to the Games.

Rose retired from competitive swimming in 1964 with a haul of Olympic medals which included four golds, a silver and a bronze.

While in the US, Rose acted in a number of movies and sometimes can be seen on late-night television in such movies as *Ride the Wild Surf* and *Ice Station Zebra*.

When Irishman Ron Delaney won the 1500 metres on the track at Melbourne in 1956 he immediately fell to his knees and it was assumed he was in severe pain. This was not the case! He was deep in prayer.

WOMEN AT THE OLYMPIC GAMES

Women have been given a raw deal in terms of participation at the modern Olympic Games. In fact the founder of the modern Games, Pierre de Coubertin, believed women should not have the right to compete unless they could hold their own with men.

By the time the second Games had rolled around, in 1900, women did manage to participate in two sports, tennis and golf, but it was merely token representation. History records that Charlotte Cooper became the first female Olympic champion when she won a gold medal in tennis.

Twelve years later swimming was added to the program and Australia's own Fanny Durack won the first gold in that discipline.

In 1924 the International Olympic Committee decided to implement more involvement for women but as is often the case with this august body, it took some time before the program was expanded. Even as late as 1936 in Berlin, there were only four sports open to the female gender.

Things moved a little faster after the Second World War and by the Mexico City Games of 1968 there were six sports for women. These were track and field, swimming, fencing, gymnastics, canoeing and volleyball.

At the time of the 1996 Olympics, women athletes could take part in twenty-three sports and this figure has been added to by the inclusion of triathlon and women's water polo for Sydney.

Australia's women have certainly delivered their share of the spoils in terms of medals. Our swimmers Dawn Fraser and Shane Gould and athletes Marjorie Jackson, Shirley Strickland and Betty Cuthbert are at the fore when it comes to counting gold medals.

ORIGINS OF THE MARATHON

The marathon, which has been on every Olympic program since 1896, commemorates an event which took place in ancient times.

In 490 BC, an Athenian army led by Miltiades defeated the Persians. Following the victory at Marathon, Miltiades asked one of his star runners, Pheidippides, to take the news of the triumph to the citizens of Athens.

Legend has it that Pheidippides ran from Marathon to Athens, a distance of approximately twenty-four miles, shouted the words 'Rejoice for we have conquered!' and then collapsed and died. The accuracy of this has never been verified but it surely embodies the spirit of the Olympic Games.

Of the eighteen men in the USSR soccer squad at the Melbourne Games, only one, Ukrainian Vadym Tyshchenko, was not from Russia. The Soviet team won the gold medal beating Yugoslavia 1–0 in the final.

FIRST AUSTRALIAN WOMAN ON THE TRACK

When the track and field events were first opened up to women in 1928, Australia chose only one female to attend the Amsterdam Games. Edith Robinson competed in both the 100- and 800-metre sprints and unfortunately did not manage to get a medal.

But her presence on the team presented a problem.

On the long trip over to Europe by ship, the team manager, Mr Les Duff, was approached by the chaperone of the team, Mrs Mabel Springfield, to inquire if Miss Robinson could be massaged by a Mr Horton who was a masseur. Duff refused! He was then told that Robinson was used to being massaged by a male in Australia. Could he not see fit to allow this to happen.

The problem was solved when Duff agreed, only with the understanding that the chaperone would be present each time a massage was required. According to Duff's official report, 'This was done in every instance'!

When the Games of 1916 were cancelled due to the hostilities of World War I, many predicted the end of this peaceful competition, but some eighty years on, the Games are still in existence, bigger and brighter than ever.

OLYMPIC SUPERLATIVES

The name of the youngest male to win an Olympic gold medal is unknown.

He was a French lad, aged somewhere between 7-10, and he was the 'drafted' cox of the Dutch team in the coxed pairs at the second Olympic Games, held in Paris in 1900.

The youngest female to win gold was Marjorie Gestring who, in 1936, won the women's springboard diving event at the Berlin Games. This young American lass was only thirteen years and 268 days when she took out the Olympic title.

The records show that the oldest male to achieve Olympic glory was Oscar Swahn. Oscar was a member of the victorious Running Deer Shooting Team from Sweden at the 1912 Games held in his native country. He was sixty-four years and 257 days.

The oldest female gold medallist was Liselott Linsenhoff from France. Miss Linsenhoff was forty-three years and thirteen days old when she won the dressage section of the equestrian events at the Munich Olympics in 1972.

The Italians spent around $30 million to ready the city of Rome for the 1960 Games. Four years later, the Japanese spent more than $2 billion to get their capital, Tokyo, prepared for the first Asian Olympics.

SUSIE O'NEILL

Every Australian gold medal performance is special, but the victory by Susie O'Neill in Atlanta was particularly pleasing to this writer. In fact, the only other one which gave me the goose bumps which I had experienced when I won in 1964, was the performance by Jon Sieben in Los Angeles. You see, both these athletes won the premier event on the whole Olympic program—the 200-metre butterfly.

The women's 200 'fly is on the last night of swimming at an Olympic Games. By the time it had rolled around in Atlanta, Australia had managed to win two silver and five bronze medals in the pool but the elusive gold had not come our way.

We had two chances that night. One was in the form of Kieren Perkins in the 1500 free and the other was Susie O'Neill in the 200 'fly.

The odds on Kieren backing up his Barcelona win were astronomical. He was swimming poorly and had only qualified eighth for the final so most people were writing him off. With hindsight, I'm sure they'll never do that again.

But Susie was up first and she had to face the Irish swimmer Michelle Smith who was seeking to win her fourth gold medal.

Susie swam the perfect race. Her coach, Scott Volkers, had said to approach the swim as four separate 50s and this she did. As the case with all 200-metre events, the third lap is crucial, and it was on this lap that O'Neill, along with her team-mate Petria Thomas, held off the challenge from Smith.

At the end of 2 minutes 7.76 seconds of power swimming, this delightful, unassuming Queensland blonde, with the magic smile, touched the wall and saw her name go up with the number '1' beside it. She was the Olympic champion. Second place went to

Thomas in 2 minutes 9.82 seconds and Smith was relegated to third.

On that night there was much joy in the Australian camp. Kieren was to achieve that marvellous win in the 1500. But for my money, the victory of the night was Susie in the 200 'fly. She had become the first female bananabender to win an individual Olympic gold medal in the swimming pool.

> In 1976 Anita DeFrantz was a member of the USA's third-placed team in the rowing eights. Ten years later she became the first black woman to be selected for membership on the International Olympic Committee.

AUSTRALIAN TEAMS AT SUMMER OLYMPIC GAMES

Year	Venue	Team Size
1896	Athens, Greece	1
1900	Paris, France	3
1904	St Louis, USA	2
1906	Athens, Greece	4
1908	London, England	25
1912	Stockholm, Sweden	22
1920	Antwerp, Belgium	13
1924	Paris, France	38
1928	Amsterdam, Holland	18
1932	Los Angeles, USA	12
1936	Berlin, Germany	34
1948	London, England	77
1952	Helsinki, Finland	85
1956	Melbourne, Australia	291
1960	Rome, Italy	211
1964	Tokyo, Japan	255
1968	Mexico City, Mexico	113
1972	Munich, Germany	170
1976	Montreal, Canada	185
1980	Moscow, USSR	125
1984	Los Angeles, USA	250
1988	Seoul, South Korea	267
1992	Barcelona, Spain	290
1996	Atlanta, USA	425